luxurious
jam

make yourself mini pots in the microwave

sonia allison

foulsham

LONDON • NEW YORK • SYDNEY • TORONTO

foulsham

The Publishing House, Bennetts Close,
Cippenham, Berkshire, SL1 5AP, England

ISBN 0-572-03030-4

Sonia Allison would like to thank Magimix for Le Duo, a combined juice extractor and citrus press, Ocean Spray Cranberries for their help with fruit, and Geraldine Hoad of the Joint Food Safety and Standards Group at the Ministry of Agriculture, Fisheries and Food for her help and advice on flavoured oils.

We have not included flavoured oils in this book because home-made preparations of this type have been implicated in cases of a serious form of food poisoning called botulism. The bacteria that causes botulism may be present on plant material such as garlic or herbs and when these are placed in oil, the bacteria may grow and produce a toxin. Commercial preparations should have been treated such that the bacteria is prevented from producing toxin; however, this would be difficult to duplicate in the domestic kitchen. The UK Government therefore does not recommend that flavoured oils be produced in the home.

Artwork: Alison Jeffrey
Cover photograph © Alan Newnham
Photographs: David Murray
Styling: Sandra Schneider and Clare Carter

Printed in Great Britain by St Edmundsbury Press, Bury St Edmunds, Suffolk.

Contents

Introduction

Welcome to a whole new creative concept in the kitchen: Fortnum & Mason meets Mrs Beeton!

How many times have you treated yourself to a jar of those extravagantly expensive and exotic jams or chutneys on display in the best supermarkets and stores? Or perhaps you have received one for a Christmas or thank-you gift. You know the sort of thing: Middle Eastern Fig and Honey Jam with Lemon, or Strawberry and Star Fruit Preserve with Grenadine.

With *Luxurious Jam*, you can create those amazing recipes – and many, many more – in your own kitchen with not much more than a large bowl, a wooden spoon, and that microwave which you often wish didn't take up so much space when you only use it for reheating and baked potatoes.

What's more, you can forget that out-dated image of vats of blackberries bubbling on the stove – after all, who wants to have only one choice of marmalade for breakfast or jam for your scones throughout the year? All these intriguing and delicious recipes are designed so that you make just one or two pots at a time. That way you can try out all sorts of exotic flavour combinations without ending up with more pots of jam than you can eat.

Fun to make, delicious to eat, and great as unusual and personal gifts – dust off your microwave and give them a try! It could be the start of a fascinating and deliciously rewarding new hobby.

High-tech Luxury Preserves

There are so many advantages to creating unique preserves in the microwave, that it's difficult to know where to start, but the sensible, small quantities must be a good option. Added to that, there is minimal mess since, as long as you follow the simple instructions, spillage and boiling over does not present a problem and little or nothing sticks and burns on to the cooking utensils. You won't get a hot, steamed-up kitchen, and smells are contained within the microwave. Heavy pans to scour are a thing of the past, while the interior of the microwave is easily wiped clean with a soft cloth.

Using the microwave gives you total and safe control as you can stop the cooking instantly at the press of a button or by opening the microwave door. And don't forget that power costs are much lower than with conventional cooking. Microwave preserves form hardly any of the scum you find when you cook on the stove, so there's no need to remedy the problem by stirring in butter at the end of cooking.

Finally, of course, the results are stunning! The flavour of the preserves retains the freshness and quality of the original ingredients and the colours stay clear and bright. You can take advantage of the vast range of unusual ingredients now so readily available in the supermarkets.

All the recipes in the book have been tested on a microwave with a full-power wattage of 750–800 watts, a roast or medium setting of 550 watts and a defrost, simmer or medium-low setting of 170–300 watts. Before you start to cook, check the settings on your own microwave and make sure you use the correct one for the each recipe. Make a note in the front of the book for reference so you won't have to look them up again.

Equipment and Utensils

A well-equipped kitchen will already have everything you need to make your luxury preserves.

Use a large, shatterproof glass bowl for cooking. It should **not** exceed 4 litres/7 pts/ 17½ cups in capacity. If you prefer, you can use a light-coloured, lightweight plastic bowl but it must be suitable for microwave use. Do not use Melamine as it absorbs heat, becomes uncomfortably hot to handle and slows down the cooking process. A china-type bowl, with no metal trims, may also be used if you don't mind the weight.

Use a wooden spoon for stirring, never metal as the handle may become overheated and burn your hand. Avoid plastic and rubber spatulas as they could disintegrate in the heat of the preserve. When stirring, always protect your hand with an oven glove in case the hot mixture splashes on to your hand. Have a plate or spoon rest near the microwave on which to lay the spoon between stirrings.

If you are making jellies, you will need a fine jelly bag or a very fine nylon sieve (strainer).

You'll also need a few saucers on to which to spoon a little of the preserve – again using your wooden spoon – to test whether it has reached setting point.

You'll need an adequate supply of jars, and it's a good idea to make a habit of collecting suitable glass jars so you always have them ready when you feel creative. Don't make the preserve first and then search for jars! If you are making chutney or other preserves containing vinegar or lemon juice, do not use jars with metal lids as the vinegar will react with the metal. Some commercial pickle jars have plastic-coated lids, and these are fine.

For some recipes, you'll need a square of muslin to hold stones (pits) or spices. For some of the chutneys, pickles and salsas, an opened-out large paper coffee filter bag, wrapped securely round the herbs and spices, is just as effective as a parcel of muslin, provided there are no sharp pieces to pierce the paper.

It is easier to fill jars without getting a messy work surface and sticky jars if you use a wide-necked funnel and a ladle. Standing the jars on a sheet of newspaper also makes clearing up easier.

Packets of jam pot covers, as they are called for preserves, are readily available in two sizes for large and small jars. Top the hot preserve with one of the greaseproof (waxed) paper discs you'll find inside each packet and cover with the lid, or cellophane secured with an elastic band, only when the preserve is completely cold (otherwise expect mildew).

Ingredients

Fruit and vegetables should always be good quality and in good condition and fruit should be just ripe. Squashy and over-ripe produce will result in mildew and a poor set. The only exception here is garden windfalls, which are inevitably damaged as they fall but quite satisfactory to use if the bruised patches are cut away and the fruit is still fresh.

Because of the risk of pesticide residue, all shop-bought fruit and vegetables should be washed thoroughly and dried before use. You can opt for organic produce but it should still be rinsed well in case it has been handled by other customers.

For some recipes, removes stones (pits) during preparation to save time. The methods give full instructions.

To ensure a good set and for a slightly shorter cooking time, the best sugar to use is jam sugar, which is granulated sugar with added natural pectin and citric acid, although in some instances – marmalade, for example – ordinary granulated sugar gives satisfactory results. Preserving sugar didn't work for me because its larger granules took too long to dissolve in the microwave and in some cases stayed in crystals, despite being thoroughly stirred; but you can use it if you are careful to make sure the sugar has fully dissolved before you proceed with the recipe. Brown sugars are fine for chutneys and pickles and different kinds have been recommended throughout the book where appropriate.

Prepared Weight Equivalents of Purchased or Picked Fruit and Vegetables

Unless otherwise specified, the amounts in the recipes are for the purchased or picked weight of ingredients. These charts show you approximately how much your purchased or picked ingredients will yield in prepared weights.

Fruit or vegetable	Purchased or picked weight	Prepared weight
Apples (and other fruit with pips)	900 g/2 lb	700 g/1½ lb peeled, cored and sliced
Apricots	900 g/2 lb	700 g/1½ lb stoned (pitted)
Banana	175 g/6 oz (2 medium)	100 g/4 oz peeled
Beetroot (red beet)	900 g/2 lb	850 g/1 lb 14 oz peeled
Blackberries (and other berries on stalks or with hulls)	900 g/2 lb	850 g/1 lb 14 oz stalked and hulled
Blueberries	No waste	
Cabbage	900 g/2 lb	850 g/1 lb 14 oz trimmed and cored
Carrots	900 g/2 lb	750 g/1¾ lb peeled
Celery	900 g/2 lb	850 g/1 lb 14 oz trimmed
Cranberries	No waste	
Cucumber	900 g/2 lb (2 large)	750 g/1¾ lb peeled
Damsons	900 g/2 lb	700 g/1½ lb stoned (pitted)
Fennel	900 g/2 lb	750 g/1¾ lb trimmed
Gooseberries	Minimal waste	
Grapes on stalks	900 g/2 lb	850 g/1 lb 14 oz

Fruit or vegetable	Purchased or picked weight	Prepared weight
Greengages	900 g/2 lb	700 g/1½ lb stoned (pitted)
Leeks	900 g/2 lb	600 g/1 lb 5 oz trimmed
Mango	700 g/1½ lb (2 large)	350 g/12 oz stoned (pitted) and peeled
Melon (ogen, cantaloupe, honeydew)	900 g/2 lb (1 large)	600 g/1 lb 5 oz seeded and peeled
Nectarines	900 g/2 lb	700 g/1½ lb stoned (pitted)
Onions	900 g/2 lb	850 g/1 lb 14 oz peeled and trimmed
Papaya	675 g/1½ lb (1 large)	350 g/12 oz seeded and peeled
Peaches	900 g/2 lb	700 g/1½ lb stoned (pitted)
Pears	900 g/2 lb	700 g/1½ lb peeled, cored and sliced
Peppers (bell peppers)	900 g/2 lb (8 medium)	750 g/1¾ lb seeded and trimmed
Persimmon	Minimal waste	
Physalis	Minimal waste	
Pineapple	900 g/2 lb (1 medium)	550 g/1¼ lb peeled and cored
Plums (and other stone fruit)	900 g/2 lb	700 g/1½ lb stoned (pitted)
Quinces	900 g/2 lb	700 g/1½ lb peeled, cored and sliced
Raspberries	900 g/2 lb	850 g/1 lb 14 oz stalked and hulled
Rhubarb	900 g/2 lb	800 g/1 lb 12 oz trimmed
Star fruit	Minimal waste	
Strawberries	900 g/2 lb	850 g/1 lb 14 oz stalked and hulled
Tomatoes	900 g/2 lb	850 g/1 lb 14 oz skinned and hulled
Watermelon	900 g/2 lb (1 medium)	450 g/1 lb seeded and skinned

Cooking Preserves in the Microwave

Before you start, collect together all your equipment and ingredients so you have everything handy when you need it. Put a couple of saucers into the fridge so they are ready when you need them to test the jam.

To sterilise jars, put 45 ml/3 tbsp of water into each one and heat on Full (750–800w) for 1½–2 minutes. Turn the jars upside-down on kitchen paper (paper towels) to drain.

When making preserves conventionally on a hob, you start off on a high heat and reduce the heat as the mixture boils to prevent it rising in the pan and boiling over. The same technique applies to microwave preserves. Many are started off on Full for 10 minutes or so, then the remaining cooking time is at a lower wattage, usually 550 to cover Roast or Medium settings. (This technique may contradict the method given in the instruction book supplied with your microwave.) Do not keep the mixture cooking at Full all the time otherwise the jam could easily boil over.

Wipe up spillages immediately with a cloth dipped in hot, soapy water, then dry with a tea towel (dish cloth). Always keep a clean tea towel handy to wipe up the condensation that builds up inside the microwave during the cooking cycle and which may need to be removed when you open the door to stir the jam.

To test if a jam, jelly, marmalade or conserve has set within the recommended cooking time, spoon a little on to a cold saucer and leave in a cool place or in the fridge for 1 minute. If a skin forms on top which wrinkles when touched, the preserve is ready.

It is important to leave jam to rest in the bowl for a little while after it has finished cooking, especially if it contains pieces of whole fruit like berries and citrus peel. If it's bottled hot, the fruit and peel will sink to the bottom; if left until lukewarm, they will stay in suspension. Use this time to warm your jars, if necessary.

Most of the recipes specify pouring into warm jars when the preserve is ready. To warm jars quickly, put an egg cup of cold water into the microwave and arrange three jars upright on the turntable in a triangle. Heat on Full for 1 minute.

Stand the jars on a sheet of newspaper to catch any drips and use a ladle to spoon the preserve into the jars through a wide-necked funnel. Top with a disc of greaseproof (waxed) paper.

Always leave the jam until cold before putting on the lids or covering with cellophane secured with an elastic band. Remember to label the jars with the name of the preserve and the date.

Store the filled jars in the coolest, driest and darkest place you have available. This will prevent colour and flavour loss as well as mildew. If you don't have a cellar or cold pantry –

rare in modern centrally-heated homes – you may need to use a garage or unheated room for storage, or even a refrigerator if you have enough space.

Making in small quantities means that you are unlikely to keep your preserves for a long time. However, if you do store them, check them frequently for mildew and spoilage, just in case. If they have spoiled, they should be thrown away.

Dried Herbs

Ever-useful to have on hand throughout the seasons, the microwave makes an excellent job of drying herbs, which stay fresh-smelling and fragrant in well-stoppered jars for many months. You can use this method to dry any fresh herbs in good condition and get great results every time.

Pull the herb leaves, or needles if you are drying rosemary, off their stems and pack them loosely into a 300 ml/½ pt/1¼ cup capacity measuring jug, filling it almost to overflowing. Rinse gently under cold running water and drain thoroughly. Pat dry between the folds of a clean tea towel (dish cloth).

Tip out in a single layer on to a double thickness of kitchen paper (paper towels), placed directly on the microwave turntable. Leave uncovered and heat on Medium (550w) for 7–8 minutes, gently moving the herbs round on the paper two or three times so that they dry evenly. As soon as they lose their bright green colour and begin to make a rustling sound like autumn (fall) leaves, you can take it that the herbs have dried out sufficiently. If not, allow a further 1–2 minutes.

Leave the herbs to cool on the paper, then crumble them between finger and thumb and spoon into jars or bottles with airtight stoppers. Store in a cool, dark place for up to three months.

Dried Citrus Peel

Use this method for making dried peel from oranges, lemons, clementines or any other similar citrus fruits. The peel can be used in sweet and savoury cooking instead of essences and extracts.

Wash and dry six clementines or any other loose-skinned citrus fruit, four medium lemons or three medium oranges. Thinly pare off the peel with a sharp vegetable peeler, avoiding the pith.

Place the peel in a single layer on a plate. Cover with kitchen paper (paper towels) and heat on Medium (550w) for 11–13 minutes until the skins look and feel dry and papery.

Leave to cool, then transfer to airtight jars and store for up to four months. Grind to a fairly fine powder before use.

Using the Microwave Safely

Never leave a preserve to cook unattended in case it bubbles up in the bowl and boils over. It should be watched over and stirred fairly frequently, with only a few minutes between, and if it looks as though it's reaching the top of the bowl and might go over the sides, open the door at once and leave the mixture to fall back into the bowl before resuming cooking.

If you are interrupted while you are cooking – by the doorbell, the phone, a child coming in, or whatever – switch off the microwave before attending to the interruption.

Always use a wooden spoon for stirring and protect your hand with an oven glove in case the hot jam splashes on to your skin. If this happens, rinse the skin in cold water until the feeling of heat goes away.

When removing the bowl of hot preserve from the microwave, always do so with hands protected by oven gloves. This is because the preserve heats the bowl, which might then be too hot to handle in comfort.

Preserves as Gifts

One flick through the enticing recipes in this book will have you itching to try out as many of these delicious preserves as possible, so there is a distinct danger that you will end up with more than you can actually eat! Of course, by definition, they are meant to last – but not for ever. And, since many of you will already have experienced the extra pleasure of giving or receiving a hand-made gift, you will know how special that makes the present – whether it is for Christmas, or a birthday, or to say welcome home, get well soon or thank you. Others may already have spotted a fundraising possibility: a stall of exotic hand-made preserves for the school Christmas fair or local fête should get a lot of custom.

If your intention is that your lovingly made preserves stay in their jars for as short a time a possible – and that will certainly be the case with many of them – you will simply want to find appropriate containers. If you have decided to give your exotic preserves as gifts, however, a little extra thought for the presentation will make all the difference. It doesn't have to take a lot of time or effort. Keep it neat and simple and you'll impress even yourself with how professional it looks.

Jars, Bottles and Containers

When you are collecting used jars for your preserves instead of putting them in the bottle bank, select ones of a useful size with sufficiently wide necks. If you put jam in a very large jar, for example, it's sticky business getting to the bottom. Jars of about 450 g/1 lb capacity are just right. Some have more interesting shapes than others, so reserve the best ones for your gifts.

Many lids will be plain-coloured and unprinted, which is ideal. If they are not, buy a few tiny tins of non-toxic paint suitable for metal surfaces from your toy or model shop and give the lids a coat of colour over the outside.

When you are looking round kitchen shops, keep an eye out for interesting jars and bottles. If you are buying coloured glass, bear in mind that you might mask the stunning colours and textures of your preserve, which may not be the best effect. Don't forget that the stopper must keep the preserve air-tight.

Ceramic jars can also be attractive, and if you are able to find something that matches the recipient's existing crockery or decor, so much the better.

Jam Pot Covers

Old-fashioned jam pot covers – circles of pretty fabric to cover the jar lid – are simple to make for an extra-special effect. Use scraps of lightweight material to match the colour of the preserve. If you don't sew and don't have any odd pieces of fabric, look out for tiny remnants or packages for patchwork, which you will find in fabric or craft stores, and pieces of narrow edging lace.

Cut out a circle of fabric about the size of a tea plate, say 17 cm/6½ in in diameter. Machine or hand sew a piece of lace round the edge, stretching the fabric slightly as you do so to make sure the lace lays flat on the curved edge of the fabric. Either simply use a strong elastic band to hold the cover on to the neck of the jar, or sew a piece of narrow elastic round the cover about 2 cm/³⁄₄ in from the edge, depending on the size of the jar. Stretch the elastic as you sew so that it gathers the fabric evenly. Cut the elastic long enough to fit snugly round the neck of the jar, allowing a little to overlap and secure the ends. That's it!

Labelling your Gifts

You should always label your jam or chutney – whether or not it is for a gift – with the recipe name and the date you made it. It can also be useful to jot a use-by date in the corner in case you forget how long it should keep. If you are packing the preserve as a gift, it can be helpful to add a few words of serving suggestions: 'great with barbecued or grilled (broiled) meats', or 'a rich, chunky breakfast marmalade', for example.

Instead of just a plain sticky label, be a bit more adventurous when you are labelling your gift jars. Attractive, decorated sticky labels for preserves or home-made wine are readily available in shops that sell kitchen and wine-making equipment, and you can make the labels look extra-special by writing with gold, silver, metallic or attractively coloured pens.

If you want something totally original, you could invest in a pack of waterproof marker pens and create your own designs. Stencils make simple and attractive patterns if you don't think you are good enough to draw freehand. Or, if you have a PC, take a look at the clip art and see if there is anything suitable. If you have a scanner with your computer system, you could even scan in a picture of the chef, or any other image you fancy, as the basis for your personalised label. This way, you can include all the text on the label while you are creating it.

Draw or print out your designs on to sheets of plain sticky labels, available from stationers, or on to plain card. If you are printing, a laser printer is best as it will give a waterproof result. Don't restrict yourself to a white background: there are all kinds of coloured labels and cards available, from subtle pastel colours to fluorescent yellow or pink.

Remember that labels don't have to be rectangular. Why not cut them into the shape of one of the fruits used in the recipe, or into the shape of a Christmas tree, a heart or a triangle, just to be different. Do keep the shapes simple as they will be the most effective and practical. Make sure the jar is cold and dry before sticking on the label.

Instead of sticky labels, you could use tie-on labels. Create the labels on card and cut them into interesting shapes. Punch a hole in one corner of the label and use ribbon or tape to tie it round the neck of the jar.

Ribbons and Bows

Use narrow ribbon to tie an attractive bow round the neck of the jar, or you can stick a ready-made fabric bow on to the lid or the side. There are all kinds of paper bows and decorations in stationers with which you can decorate your jars. If you use an ordinary narrow, paper gift ribbon, you can tie two or three strands around the neck of the jar, leaving long ends. Pull along the back of each length of ribbon end with the flat blade of a pair of scissors to curl them into spirals.

Choose colours to match your lids, labels or jams, or go sparkly and opt for silver or gold ribbon – or both.

Tassels

To make a little tassel to hang on the side of the jar, cut out two pieces of card about 13 x 20 cm/5 x 8 in. Hold the two pieces together and wind embroidery or fancy thread

around them – about fifty times if the thread if fairly thick, more if it is fine. Take a strand of the same thread about 3.7 metres/4 yards long, fold it in half and thread the loop through the eye of a large needle. Push the needle and thread under the threads at the top of the card, then pass the needle back through the loop and pull tight to secure the threads, tying to make sure they are tightly held. Cut through the threads at the bottom of the card. Wind the long thread several times around the tassel about 2.5 cm/1 in from the top, then push the needle and thread back to the top of the tassel and tie to create a thread to attach it to a label or to the jar. Trim the bottom of the tassel neatly to finish.

Wrapping the Jars

You can wrap your jars with gift paper but, since they are so attractive, it is not absolutely necessary. One way is to stand the jar in the centre of a square of cellophane, the side measurement of which should be twice the height of the jar plus about 15 cm/6 in. Bring the cellophane up over the jar and tie it on top of the lid, then decorate with curled ribbons or tassels.

New Ideas

Look out for new ideas for decorating your gifts as you flick through magazines or watch craft programmes on television. Ideas for Christmas decorations, for example, may easily be adapted as decorations for your special preserves. Your unique gifts will certainly be much in demand – so make sure you don't leave anyone off the list!

Notes on the Recipes

○ Do not mix metric, imperial and American measures. Follow one set only.

○ American terms are given in brackets.

○ All spoon measurements are level: 1 tsp = 5 ml; 1 tbsp = 15 ml.

○ Always wash, peel, core and seed, if necessary, fresh foods before use.

○ Always use fresh herbs unless dried are specifically called for. If you wish, you can substitute dried for fresh, using only half the quantity or less as they are very pungent, but chopped frozen varieties are much better than dried. There is no substitute for fresh parsley and coriander (cilantro).

○ Use your own discretion in substituting ingredients and personalising the recipes. Make notes of particular successes as you go along.

○ Use whatever kitchen gadgets you like in order to speed up preparation and cooking times: mixers for whisking, food processors for grating, slicing, mixing or kneading, blenders for liquidising.

○ Always check the wattage of your own appliance and follow the recipes accordingly.

Jams

Home-made products taste so much **fruitier** than anything shop-bought and, with these recipes, you have a selection of **luxury** jams that will rival anything you can find in the best **delicatessens.** There are some basic recipes – ideal if you have not tried jam-making before – and a whole range of more unusual and exotic jams to allow you to make the best of the availability of **unusual** fruits in season.

Apple and Blackberry Jam

An exquisite jam that heralds the onset of autumn (fall) and the last of the wild berry picking.

makes 1.25 kg/2½ lb/2 large jars

350 g/12 oz cooking (tart) apples, peeled, cored and thinly sliced
550 g/1¼ lb blackberries
120 ml/4 fl oz/½ cup boiling water
900 g/2 lb/4 cups granulated sugar

1 Put the apples and blackberries in a 4 litre/7 pt/17½ cup capacity bowl and add the boiling water. Leave uncovered and cook on Medium (550w) for about 25 minutes until both fruits are soft and well-pulped, stirring three times with a wooden spoon.

2 Stir in the sugar and cook, uncovered, on Full (750–800w) for 7 minutes until the sugar has dissolved, stirring three times.

3 Reduce the power to Medium and continue to cook for about 30 minutes until setting point is reached, stirring three or four times.

4 Allow to cool to lukewarm, then ladle into warmed jars, top with paper discs and leave until cold.

5 Cover with lids or cellophane and label the jars.

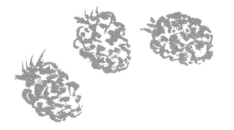

Jams should be stored in a cool, dark place and can be kept for up to a year but must be checked regularly for mildew at two-month intervals.

Apple and Quince Jam

An attractive jam with a pinky glow and an elegant flavour. Apart from spooning on the usual toast and buttered buns, this jam can also be used as a condiment to eat with lamb and duck.

makes 1.25 kg/2½ lb/2 large jars

250 g/10 oz cooking (tart) apples, peeled, cored and chopped
600 ml/1 pt/2½ cups boiling water
175 g/6 oz/1 cup quince pulp from Luxury Quince Jelly (see page 88)
   or Quince Jelly with Rose (see page 89)
30 ml/2 tbsp lemon juice
550 g/1¼ lb/2½ cups granulated sugar
120 ml/4 fl oz/½ cup liquid pectin

1 Put the apples in a 3 litre/5 pt/12½ cup capacity bowl and add half the boiling water. Leave uncovered and cook on Full (750–800w) for 10 minutes, stirring three times.

2 Stir in the quince pulp, the remaining boiling water and half the lemon juice.

3 Leave uncovered and cook on Full (750–800w) for 5 minutes, stirring once.

4 Stir in the sugar and the remaining lemon juice. Leave uncovered and cook on Full for 8 minutes until the sugar has dissolved, stirring twice with a wooden spoon.

5 Reduce the power to Medium (550w) and continue to cook for a further 25–30 minutes, stirring four times.

6 Remove from the microwave and stir in the liquid pectin.

7 Leave until almost cold and beginning to set before spooning into warmed jars. Top with paper discs, then leave until completely cold.

8 Cover with lids or cellophane and label the jars.

Apricot and Strawberry Jam with Fresh Tamarind

Fresh tamarind, also known as Indian date, is an African and Indian fruit that acts as a souring and slight flavouring agent. Related to the pea family, it looks like a small version of a broad (lima) bean with a lightish brown and brittle skin. Inside are stones (pits) or fairly large seeds naturally held together like a parcel with fibres and surrounded by flesh that resembles fresh dates in appearance and texture. They team cheerfully with apricot and strawberry and heighten the taste of the jam without being intrusive. Tamarinds are available from large supermarkets.

makes 1.5 kg/3 lb/3 jars

2 fresh tamarinds
700 g/1½ lb apricots, halved, stoned (pitted) and thinly sliced
350 g/12 oz strawberries, hulled and sliced
150 ml/¼ pt/⅔ cup boiling water
900 g/2 lb/4 cups jam sugar

1 Take the brittle skin off the tamarinds and remove the inner strings. Place the flesh in a 4 litre/7 pt/17½ cup capacity bowl with the apricots and strawberries and add the boiling water. Cover and cook on Full (750–800w) for 15 minutes, stirring once. (The tamarinds will cook down.)

2 Uncover, stir in the sugar and cook on Full for 8 minutes until the sugar has dissolved, stirring twice with a wooden spoon.

3 Reduce the power to Medium (550w) and continue to cook for 30–35 minutes until setting point is reached, stirring three or four times.

4 Allow to cool to lukewarm, remove the tamarind seeds with a spoon, then ladle into warmed jars, top with paper discs and leave until cold.

5 Cover with lids or cellophane and label the jars.

Fresh Apricot Jam with Amaretto

Glowing orange like amber, this is a firm and tangy jam with the merest hint of almond in the background.

makes 1 kg/2¼ lb/2 jars

700 g/1½ lb fresh apricots, stoned (pitted) and thickly sliced
Juice of ½ medium lemon
150 ml/¼ pt/⅔ cup boiling water
700 g/1½ lb/3 cups granulated sugar
30 ml/2 tbsp amaretto liqueur

1 Put the apricots and lemon juice in a 4 litre/7 pt/17½ cup capacity bowl and add the boiling water. Cover and cook on Full (750–800w) for 12 minutes, stirring once.

2 Uncover, mash the fruit down with a potato masher, then stir in the sugar.

3 Cook on Full for 8 minutes until the sugar has dissolved, stirring twice with a wooden spoon.

4 Reduce the power to Medium (550w) and continue to cook for a further 25–30 minutes until setting point is reached, stirring three or four times. Mix in the amaretto.

5 Allow to cool to lukewarm, then ladle into warmed jars, top with paper discs and leave until cold.

6 Cover with lids or cellophane and label the jars.

Blackcurrant Jam

This is one of Britain's finest and most popular jams – an absolute classic that is simplicity itself to make in the microwave.

makes 1.25 kg/2½ lb/2 large jars

450 g/1 lb blackcurrants, stalks removed
450 ml/¾ pt/2 cups boiling water
700 g/1½ lb/3 cups granulated sugar

1 Put the blackcurrants in a 4 litre/7 pt/17½ cup capacity bowl and add the boiling water. Cover with a lid or plate and cook on Medium (550w) for 25 minutes until tender, stirring three times with a wooden spoon.

2 Uncover and stir in the sugar. Leave uncovered and cook on Full (750–800w) for 10 minutes until the sugar has dissolved, stirring twice.

3 Reduce the power to Medium and continue to cook for a further 25–30 minutes until setting point is reached, stirring three or four times.

4 Allow to cool to lukewarm, then ladle into warmed jars, top with paper discs and leave until cold.

5 Cover with lids or cellophane and label the jars.

*Opposite: Fig, Date and Cob Nut Jam (page 32),
Mulled Red Wine Jelly (page 90) and Persimmon Butter (page 112)*

Cranberry, Apple and Grenadilla Jam

Grenadillas are tropical fruit with a hard yellow shell lined with inedible pith and filled with a seedy pulp that looks something like frog spawn. But don't be put off! Tasting faintly of elderberry, it combines superbly with cranberries and apples and produces a surprise package of a jam with a slightly crunchy texture and superb fragrance.

makes 1.6 kg/3½ lb/3 large jars

450 g/1 lb cranberries
700 g/1½ lb cooking (tart) apples, peeled, cored and sliced
2 large grenadillas
175 ml/6 fl oz/¾ cup boiling water
1 kg/2¼ lb/4½ cups jam sugar

1 Put the cranberries and apples in a 4 litre/7 pt/17½ cup capacity bowl. Crack open the grendillas and scoop the pulp into the bowl. Stir in the boiling water.

2 Leave uncovered and cook on Medium (550w) for 15 minutes, stirring once with a wooden spoon.

3 Stir in the sugar, then cook on Full (750–800w) for 7 minutes until the sugar has dissolved, stirring twice.

4 Reduce the power to Medium and cook for about 25 minutes until setting point is reached, stirring three or four times.

5 Allow to cool to lukewarm, then ladle into warmed jars, top with paper discs and leave until cold.

6 Cover with lids or cellophane and label the jars.

Opposite: *Physalis Jam (page 46)*

East-West Cranberry and Mango Jam
with Orange Flower Water

The subtle flavours of the Orient and the Caribbean combine beautifully with the scent of orange blossom in this off-beat jam.

makes 1.6 kg/3½ lb/3 large jars

450 g/1 lb cranberries

1 large just-ripe mango, about 350 g/12 oz, peeled, stoned (pitted) and diced

225 g/8 oz cooking (tart) apples, peeled, cored and coarsely chopped

1 kg/2¼ lb/4½ cups jam sugar

30 ml/2 tbsp orange flower water

1 Tip the cranberries, mango dice and apple pieces into a 4 litre/7 pt/17½ cup capacity bowl. Cover and cook on Full (750–800w) for 7 minutes, stirring twice.

2 Uncover and stir in the sugar. Cook on Full for 7 minutes until the sugar has dissolved, stirring twice with a wooden spoon.

3 Reduce the power to Medium (550w) and cook for 20 minutes, stirring three times.

4 Mix in the orange flower water and continue to cook on Medium for a further 5–6 minutes until setting point is reached.

5 Allow to cool to lukewarm, then ladle into warmed jars, top with paper discs and leave until cold.

6 Cover with lids or cellophane and label the jars.

Cranberry Jam with Blueberries

A deeply dark-red, almost velvety jam, the sharpness of the cranberries is offset by the gentler and softer-natured blueberries, which are in the shops fresh in the late autumn (fall) and winter months from South Africa and North America.

makes 1 kg/2¼ lb/2 jars

> 450 g/1 lb/2 cups granulated or jam sugar
> 450 ml/¾ pt/2 cups boiling water
> 350 g/12 oz/3 cups fresh cranberries
> 100 g/4 oz/1 cup fresh blueberries

1 Tip the sugar into a 3 litre/5 pt/12½ cup capacity bowl and add the boiling water. Leave uncovered and cook on Full (750–800w) for 6 minutes until the sugar has dissolved, stirring twice.

2 Mix in both the berries. Still uncovered, cook on Full for 10 minutes, stirring three or four times with a wooden spoon.

3 Reduce the power to Medium (550w) and continue to cook for a further 20–25 minutes until setting point is reached, stirring two or three times.

4 Allow to cool to lukewarm, then ladle into warmed jars, top with paper discs and leave until cold.

5 Cover with lids or cellophane and label the jars.

Cranberry and Apple Jam with Nectarine and Mace

A terrific flavour assortment here, this wonderful preserve is teasingly spiced with mace.

makes 1.25 kg/2½ lb/2 large jars

450 g/1 lb cranberries
1 large, sharp eating (dessert) apple, about 175 g/6 oz, peeled, cored
  and coarsely chopped
2 large nectarines, about 300 g/10 oz, halved, stoned (pitted) and chopped
1.5–2.5 ml/¼–½ tsp ground mace
900 g/2 lb/4 cups jam sugar

1 Tip the cranberries into a 4 litre/7 pt/17½ cup capacity bowl and add the apple and nectarines. Cover and cook on Medium (550w) for 20 minutes until soft and pulpy.

2 Stir in the mace and sugar, then cook on Full (750–800w) for 7 minutes until the sugar has dissolved, stirring twice with a wooden spoon.

3 Reduce the power to Medium and continue to cook for about 30 minutes until setting point is reached, stirring three or four times.

4 Allow to cool to lukewarm, then ladle into warmed jars, top with paper discs and leave until cold.

5 Cover with lids or cellophane and label the jars.

Cranberry, Tomato and Kumquat Jam with Mandarin Liqueur

A lively and colourful mix, with orange the underlying flavour. Kumquats belong to the citrus family and came originally from the Far East, being introduced to Europe in the middle of the nineteenth century. They look like miniature round or oval oranges, tend to be bitter-sweet, and the vividly orange skin is edible – all you discard is the pips. When in season, kumquats are stocked by all the major supermarket outlets. Mandarin liqueur is available in major supermarkets and off-licences (liquor stores).

makes 1 kg /2¼ lb/2 jars

175 g/6 oz kumquats, thinly sliced
1 large, firm, ripe tomato, about 100 g/4 oz, skinned and coarsely chopped
450 ml/¾ pt/2 cups boiling water
450 g/1 lb/2 cups jam sugar
200 g/7 oz cranberries
15 ml/1 tbsp mandarin liqueur

1 Place the kumquats and tomato in a 3½ litre/6 pt/15 cup capacity bowl and add the boiling water. Leave uncovered and cook on Full (750–800w) for 10 minutes.

2 Stir in the sugar and cranberries, then continue to cook on Full for 7 minutes until the sugar has dissolved, stirring twice with a wooden spoon.

3 Reduce the power to Medium (550w) and continue to cook for about 30 minutes until setting point is reached, stirring three or four times.

4 Stir in the liqueur.

5 Allow to cool to lukewarm, then ladle into warmed jars, top with paper discs and leave until cold.

6 Cover with lids or cellophane and label the jars.

Damson Jam

A deep-red jam with an assertive tartness and lingering flavour, which makes a very English preserve for the tea table. When choosing your damsons, opt for the not-too-small damson plums, which are easier to stone (pit) than the little ones, with no discernible difference in the flavour.

makes 1 kg/2¼ lb/2 jars

550 g/1¼ lb damson plums, halved and stoned (pitted)
250 ml/8 fl oz/1 cup boiling water
700 g/1½ lb/3 cups granulated sugar

1 Put the damsons in a 4 litre/7 pt/17½ cup capacity bowl and add the boiling water. Cover and cook on Medium (550w) for 10 minutes.

2 Uncover and work to a coarse pulp with a potato masher.

3 Leave uncovered and continue to cook on Medium for a further 5 minutes.

4 Stir in the sugar and cook on Full (750–800w) for 7 minutes until the sugar has dissolved, stirring twice with a wooden spoon.

5 Reduce the power to Medium and continue to cook for a further 25–30 minutes, stirring three or four times, until setting point is reached.

6 Allow to cool to lukewarm, then ladle into warmed jars, top with paper discs and leave until cold.

7 Cover with lids or cellophane and label the jars.

Damson and Rhubarb Jam

A deep-toned and chunky jam with a warm, fruity flavour and appetising sharpness.

makes 1.5 kg/3 lb/3 jars

550 g/1¼ lb damson plums, halved and stoned (pitted)
500 g/18 oz rhubarb, trimmed and cut into chunks
150 ml/¼ pt/⅔ cup boiling water
1 kg/2¼ lb/4½ cups jam sugar

1 Put the damsons and rhubarb in a 4 litre/7 pt/17½ cup capacity bowl and add the boiling water. Cover and cook on Full (750–800w) for 10 minutes, stirring once.

2 Uncover, mash down the fruit with a potato masher and stir in the sugar.

3 Cook on Full for 10 minutes until the sugar has dissolved, stirring twice with a wooden spoon.

4 Reduce the power to Medium (550w) and continue to cook for 30–35 minutes until setting point is reached, stirring three or four times.

5 Allow to cool to lukewarm, then ladle into warmed jars, top with paper discs and leave until cold.

6 Cover with lids or cellophane and label the jars.

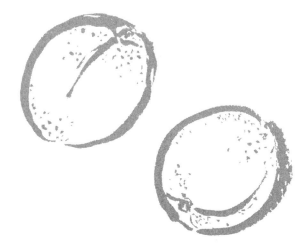

Fresh Fig, Date and Cob Nut Jam

Autumn (fall) cob nuts, also known as filberts, look like plump almonds with beige skins when shelled, although some are round and bumpy like the more familiar hazelnuts. They are juicy and crisp and make a wonderful addition to this dark pink, autumn jam. See photograph opposite page 24.

makes 1.25 kg/2½ lb/2 large jars

> 225 g/8 oz cob nuts, shelled and halved
> 450 g/1 lb fleshy figs, coarsely chopped
> 200 g/7 oz fresh dates, stoned (pitted) and coarsely chopped
> 30 ml/2 tbsp lime juice cordial
> 30 ml/2 tbsp lemon juice
> 900 g/2 lb/4 cups jam sugar

1 Put the nuts, figs, dates, lime cordial and lemon juice in a 4 litre/7 pt/17½ cup capacity bowl. Cover and cook on Full (750–800w) for 10 minutes, stirring once.

2 Uncover, stir in the sugar and cook on Full for 8 minutes until the sugar has dissolved, stirring twice with a wooden spoon.

3 Reduce the power to Medium (550w) and continue to cook for 25–30 minutes until setting point is reached, stirring three or four times.

4 Allow to cool to lukewarm, then ladle into warmed jars, top with paper discs and leave until cold.

5 Cover with lids or cellophane and label the jars.

Fresh Fig and Vanilla Jam

The natural affinity of vanilla and figs works together beautifully in this jam.

makes 900 g/2 lb/2 jars

700 g/1½ lb fleshy figs, coarsely chopped
30 ml/2 tbsp lemon juice
5 ml/1 tsp vanilla essence (extract)
700 g/1½ lb/3 cups jam sugar

1 Put the figs, lemon juice and vanilla in a 4 litre/7 pt/17½ cup capacity bowl. Cover and cook on Full (750–800w) for 7 minutes, stirring once.

2 Uncover, stir in the sugar and cook on Full for 8 minutes until the sugar has dissolved, stirring twice with a wooden spoon.

3 Reduce the power to Medium (550w) and continue to cook for 25–30 minutes until setting point is reached, stirring three or four times.

4 Allow to cool to lukewarm, then ladle into warmed jars, top with paper discs and leave until cold.

5 Cover with lids or cellophane and label the jars.

Fresh Fig and Lemon Jam

makes 900 g/2 lb/2 jars

Prepare as for Fresh Fig and Vanilla Jam, but add the finely grated (shredded) rind and juice of 1 large lemon instead of just the lemon juice.

Fresh Fig and Juniper Jam

makes 900 g/2 lb/2 jars

Prepare as for Fresh Fig and Vanilla Jam, but omit the vanilla essence (extract) and add 12 air-dried juniper berries, crushed between finger and thumb.

Sangria-style Fig Jam

The blend of flavours here is outstanding and the jam makes a memorable addition to thick yoghurt or ice cream. You can also try it as a trendy basis for fruit salad.

makes 1.75 kg/4 lb/4 jars

900 g/2 lb fleshy figs, coarsely chopped
150 ml/¼ pt/⅔ cup Spanish red wine
1 large orange
45 ml/3 tbsp lemon juice
1 kg/2¼ lb/4½ cups jam sugar

1 Put the figs in a 4 litre/7 pt/17½ cup capacity bowl with the wine.

2 Grate (shred) the rind off half the orange, then peel the orange, discarding all traces of pith, and cut the flesh into small pieces, removing the pips. Add to the bowl with the orange rind and lemon juice. Cover and cook on Full (750–800w) for 10 minutes, stirring once.

3 Uncover, stir in the sugar and cook on Full for 8 minutes until the sugar has dissolved, stirring twice with a wooden spoon.

4 Reduce the power to Medium (550w) and continue to cook for 25–30 minutes until setting point is reached, stirring three or four times.

5 Allow to cool to lukewarm, then ladle into warmed jars, top with paper discs and leave until cold.

6 Cover with lids or cellophane and label the jars.

Middle Eastern Fig and Honey Jam with Lemon

Abundantly and warmly scented with fine fragrances from Arabia, this splendid jam is a sheer joy.

makes 1.5 kg/3 lb/3 jars

900 g/2 lb fleshy figs, coarsely chopped
350 g/12 oz flower honey
60 ml/4 tbsp lemon juice
30 ml/2 tbsp rose water
550 g/1¼ lb/2½ cups jam sugar

1 Put the figs, honey, lemon juice and rose water in a 4 litre/7 pt/17½ cup capacity bowl. Cover and cook on Full (750–800w) for 10 minutes, stirring once.

2 Uncover, stir in the sugar and cook on Full for 8 minutes until the sugar has dissolved, stirring twice with a wooden spoon.

3 Reduce the power to Medium (550w) and continue to cook for 25–30 minutes until setting point is reached, stirring three or four times.

4 Allow to cool to lukewarm, then ladle into warmed jars, top with paper discs and leave until cold.

5 Cover with lids or cellophane and label the jars.

Gooseberry Jam

A delightfully sharp-flavoured jam with a bright colour.

makes 1.25 kg/2½ lb/2 large jars

900 g/2 lb gooseberries, topped and tailed
150 ml/¼ pt/⅔ cup boiling water
900 g/2 lb/4 cups granulated sugar

1 Put the gooseberries in a 4 litre/7pt/17½ cup capacity bowl and add the boiling water. Leave uncovered and cook on Medium (550w) for about 25 minutes until soft and pulpy.

2 Stir in the sugar and cook, uncovered, on Full (750–800w) for 7 minutes until the sugar has dissolved, stirring three times with a wooden spoon.

3 Reduce the power to Medium and continue to cook for about 30 minutes until setting point is reached, stirring three or four times.

4 Allow to cool to lukewarm, then ladle into warmed jars, top with paper discs and leave until cold.

5 Cover with lids or cellophane and label the jars.

Gooseberry, Rhubarb and Elderflower Jam

A truly heavenly summer jam in warm pinky gold.

makes 1.25 kg/2½ lb/2 large jars

350 g/12 oz green gooseberries, topped, tailed and halved
450 g/1 lb rhubarb, trimmed and cut into chunks
Flowers from 2 elderflower heads
150 ml/¼ pt/⅔ cup boiling water
700 g/1½ lb/3 cups caster (superfine) sugar

1 Put the gooseberries, rhubarb and elderflowers in a 4 litre/7 pt/17½ cup capacity bowl and add the boiling water. Cover and cook on Full (750–800w) for 15 minutes, stirring once.

2 Uncover, stir in the sugar and cook on Full for 8 minutes until the sugar has dissolved, stirring twice with a wooden spoon.

3 Reduce the power to Medium (550w) and continue to cook for 25 minutes until setting point is reached, stirring three or four times.

4 Allow to cool to lukewarm, then ladle into warmed jars, top with paper discs and leave until cold.

5 Cover with lids or cellophane and label the jars.

Black Grape and Gooseberry Jam with Vanilla

A striking jam with a backdrop of vanilla for originality.

makes 1 kg/2¼ lb/2 jars

350 g/12 oz gooseberries, topped, tailed and halved
350 g/12 oz seedless black grapes, removed from their stalks
30 ml/2 tbsp lemon juice
90 ml/6 tbsp boiling water
700 g/1½ lb/3 cups jam sugar
5 ml/1 tsp vanilla essence (extract)

1 Put the gooseberries, grapes and lemon juice in a 4 litre/7 pt/17½ cup capacity bowl and add the boiling water. Cover and cook on Full (750–800w) for 15 minutes, stirring once.

2 Uncover, stir in the sugar and cook on Full for 8 minutes until the sugar has dissolved, stirring twice with a wooden spoon.

3 Reduce the power to Medium (550w) and continue to cook for 30 minutes until setting point is reached, stirring three or four times.

4 Stir in the vanilla essence.

5 Allow to cool to lukewarm, then ladle into warmed jars, top with paper discs and leave until cold.

6 Cover with lids or cellophane and label the jars.

Grape Jam with Grapefruit Juice

A bewitching flavour characterises this subtle jam which boasts a warm golden green colour.

makes 1.5 kg/3 lb/3 jars

750 g/1¾ lb seedless green grapes, removed from their stalks
300 ml/½ pt/1¼ cups grapefruit juice
30 ml/2 tbsp lemon juice
1 kg/2¼ lb/4½ cups jam sugar

1 Coarsely chop the grapes in a food processor, then put in a 4 litre/7 pt/17½ cup capacity bowl with the grapefruit and lemon juices. Leave uncovered and cook on Full (750–800w) for 10 minutes, stirring once.

2 Stir in the sugar and cook on Full for 8 minutes until the sugar has dissolved, stirring twice with a wooden spoon.

3 Reduce the power to Medium (550w) and continue to cook for 30 minutes until setting point is reached, stirring three or four times.

4 Allow to cool to lukewarm, then ladle into warmed jars, top with paper discs and leave until cold.

5 Cover with lids or cellophane and label the jars.

Greengage Jam

This must surely rate as one of the all-time greats, a deeply golden-green jam with a majestic flavour.

makes 1.25 kg/2½ lb/2 large jars

> 900 g/2 lb greengages, halved and stoned (pitted)
> 75 ml/5 tbsp boiling water
> 700 g/1½ lb/3 cups granulated sugar

1 Put the greengages in a 4 litre/7 pt/17½ cup capacity bowl and add the boiling water. Leave uncovered and cook on Full (750–800w) for 10 minutes, stirring once.

2 Stir in the sugar and continue to cook on Full for 7–8 minutes until the sugar has dissolved, stirring three times with a wooden spoon.

3 Reduce the power to Medium (550w) and continue to cook for 25–30 minutes until setting point is reached, stirring three or four times.

4 Allow to cool to lukewarm, then ladle into warmed jars, top with paper discs and leave until cold.

5 Cover with lids or cellophane and label the jars.

Red Plum Jam

makes 1.25 kg/2½ lb/2 large jars

Prepare as for Greengage Jam, but substitute red plums for the greengages.

Greengage, Apricot and Nectarine Jam

You can vary the proportions of the fruits to suit your own taste.

makes 1.25 kg/2½ lb/2 large jars

450 g/1 lb greengages, halved and stoned (pitted)
225 g/8 oz apricots, halved, stoned (pitted) and sliced
2 large nectarines, halved, stoned (pitted) and sliced
150 ml/¼ pt/⅔ cup boiling water
700 g/1½ lb/3 cups jam sugar

1 Put all the fruit in a 4 litre/7 pt/17½ cup capacity bowl and add the boiling water. Leave uncovered and cook on Full (750–800w) for 10 minutes.

2 Stir in the sugar and continue to cook on Full for 7–8 minutes until the sugar has dissolved, stirring three times with a wooden spoon.

3 Reduce the power to Medium (550w) and continue to cook for 25–30 minutes until setting point is reached, stirring three or four times.

4 Allow to cool to lukewarm, then ladle into warmed jars, top with paper discs and leave until cold.

5 Cover with lids or cellophane and label the jars.

Mango Jam with Orange

A bouquet of striking flavours characterises this tropical jam.

makes 1.25 kg/2½ lb/2 large jars

6 medium–large, slightly under-ripe mangoes, about 1.5 kg/3 lb, peeled and
   stoned (pitted)
150 ml/¼ pt/⅔ cup boiling water
30 ml/2 tbsp lemon juice
700 g/1½ lb/3 cups jam sugar
30 ml/2 tbsp orange liqueur

1 Coarsely chop the mango flesh and put in a 4 litre/7 pt/17½ cup capacity bowl with
the boiling water and lemon juice. Cover and cook on Full (750–800w) for 10 minutes,
stirring once.

2 Uncover, stir in the sugar and cook on Full for 8 minutes until the sugar has dissolved,
stirring twice with a wooden spoon.

3 Reduce the power to Medium (550w) and continue to cook for a further 25 minutes
until setting point is reached, stirring three or four times.

4 Stir in the orange liqueur.

5 Allow to cool to lukewarm, then ladle into warmed jars, top with paper discs and
leave until cold.

6 Cover with lids or cellophane and label the jars.

Mixed Melon Jam

Splashed with Japan's bright green Midori melon liqueur, this is a novelty jam that is mild in flavour and attractively golden yellow in colour. If you cannot find Midori liqueur, use another fruit liqueur instead.

makes 1.5 kg/3 lb/3 jars

750 g/1¾ lb cantaloupe melon, peeled, seeded and diced
750 g/1¾ lb honeydew melon, peeled, seeded and diced
15 ml/3 tbsp lemon juice
900 g/2 lb/4 cups jam sugar
30 ml/2 tbsp Midori melon liqueur

1 Put the melon flesh and lemon juice in a 4 litre/7 pt/17½ cup capacity bowl. Leave uncovered and cook on Full (750–800w) for 7 minutes.

2 Stir in the sugar, then cook on Full for a further 7 minutes until the sugar has dissolved, stirring twice with a wooden spoon.

3 Reduce the power to Medium (550w) and continue to cook for about 30 minutes until setting point is reached, stirring three or four times.

4 Stir in the liqueur.

5 Allow to cool to lukewarm, then ladle into warmed jars, top with paper discs and leave until cold.

6 Cover with lids or cellophane and label the jars.

Melon, Strawberry and Lime Jam

A fine-tasting, light red jam with a subtle hint of lime. It's a stunner as a plain cake filling with whipped cream or spread over pancakes. See photograph opposite page 48.

makes 1.25 kg/2½ lb/2 large jars

350 g/12 oz strawberries, hulled and halved

900 g/2 lb pink watermelon, peeled, seeded and cubed

Grated (shredded) rind and juice of 1 lime

15 ml/1 tbsp lemon juice

750 g/1¾ lb/3½ cups jam sugar

1 Put the strawberries, melon flesh and lime rind and juice in a 4 litre/7 pt/ 17½ cup capacity bowl. Cover and cook on Full (750–800w) for 10 minutes.

2 Uncover and mix in the lemon juice and sugar. Cook on Full for a further 8 minutes until the sugar has dissolved, stirring twice with a wooden spoon.

3 Reduce the power to Medium (550w) and continue to cook for a further 25–30 minutes until setting point is reached, stirring three or four times.

4 Allow to cool to lukewarm, then ladle into warmed jars, top with paper discs and leave until cold.

5 Cover with lids or cellophane and label the jars.

Winter Jam

A coming together of early winter fruits makes for an off-beat jam with a deliciously unusual after-taste.

makes 1.25 kg/2½ lb/2 large jars

2 large ripe persimmons, about 450 g/1 lb, coarsely chopped
2 large dessert pears, about 225 g/8 oz, peeled and diced
1 medium banana, about 175 g/6 oz, thinly sliced
45 ml/3 tbsp lemon juice
150 ml/¼ pt/⅔ cup boiling water
700 g/1½ lb/3 cups jam sugar

1 Put all the fruit in a 4 litre/7 pt/17½ cup capacity bowl. Add 30 ml/2 tbsp of the lemon juice and the water. Leave uncovered and cook on Full (750–800w) for 5 minutes.

2 Stir in the sugar, leave uncovered and cook on Full for 5 minutes until the sugar has dissolved, stirring twice with a wooden spoon.

3 Reduce the power to Medium (550w) and continue to cook a further 30–35 minutes until setting point is reached, stirring three or four times with a wooden spoon.

4 Stir in the remaining lemon juice and continue to cook on Medium for a further 7 minutes.

5 Allow to cool to lukewarm, then ladle into warmed jars, top with paper discs and leave until cold.

6 Cover with lids or cellophane and label the jars.

Physalis Jam

Also known as the Cape gooseberry, physalis is a member of the tomato family and came originally from South America, though it's now grown in many other of the world's hot spots including South Africa, from where it takes its other name. The fruit grows as yellow, cherry-sized berries enclosed by thin, papery, parchment-coloured loose husks and they have a unique quality and flavour. Although expensive, it is definitely worth making physalis jam at least once in a lifetime! See photograph opposite page 25.

makes 700 g/1½ lb/2 small jars

> 450 g/1 lb physalis, husks removed and halved
> 150 ml/¼ pt/⅔ cup boiling water
> 450 g/1 lb/2 cups granulated sugar

1 Put the physalis in a 3 litre/5 pt/12½ cup capacity bowl and add the boiling water. Cover and cook on Medium (550w) for 10 minutes, stirring once.

2 Stir in the sugar and cook on Medium for 12 minutes until the sugar has dissolved, stirring twice with a wooden spoon.

3 Continue to cook on Medium for 15–20 minutes until setting point is reached, stirring three or four times.

4 Allow to cool to lukewarm, then ladle into warmed jars, top with paper discs and leave until cold.

5 Cover with lids or cellophane and label the jars.

Pineapple Jam

A finely flavoured, golden jam which is easy to make and a change from more traditional preserves.

makes 700 g/1½ lb/2 small jars

1 medium–large pineapple, about 900 g/2 lb, peeled and with eyes removed
550 g/1¼ lb/2½ cups jam sugar
15 ml/1 tbsp lemon juice

1 Slice the pineapple thickly, then cut each slice into chunks. Grind to a coarse purée (paste) in a food processor.

2 Place in a 4 litre/7 pt/17½ cup capacity bowl. Stir in the sugar and lemon juice and leave to stand for 1 hour.

3 Leave uncovered and cook on Full (750–800w) for 6 minutes until the sugar has dissolved, stirring twice with a wooden spoon.

4 Reduce the power to Medium (550w) and continue to cook for a further 25–30 minutes until setting point is reached, stirring three or four times.

5 Allow to cool to lukewarm, then ladle into warmed jars, top with paper discs and leave until cold.

6 Cover with lids or cellophane and label the jars.

Bird of Paradise Pineapple Jam

Deep orangey-pink and with a delicious taste, this jam can also be used as a condiment and is a lively addition to the cheese board. It has a slight astringency to it, characteristic of persimmons.

makes 1.25 kg/2½ lb/2 large jars

1 medium pineapple, about 900 g/2 lb, peeled and with eyes removed
1 medium cooking (tart) apple, about 100 g/4 oz, peeled, cored and quartered
1 large persimmon, about 225 g/8 oz, coarsely chopped with skin
5 ml/1 tsp grated (shredded) lime rind
Juice of 1 medium lemon
150 ml/¼ pt/⅔ cup boiling water
725 g/1 lb 10 oz/3¼ cups jam sugar

1 Slice the pineapple, then cut each slice into six wedges. Place in a food processor with the apple and grind coarsely.

2 Transfer to a 4 litre/7 pt/17½ cup capacity bowl and add the persimmon, lime rind, lemon juice and boiling water. Leave uncovered and cook on Full (750–800w) for 5 minutes.

3 Stir in the sugar, leave uncovered and cook on Full for 5 minutes until the sugar has dissolved, stirring twice with a wooden spoon.

4 Reduce the power to Medium (550w) and continue to cook a further 30–35 minutes until setting point is reached, stirring three or four times with a wooden spoon.

5 Allow to cool to lukewarm, then ladle into warmed jars, top with paper discs and leave until cold.

6 Cover with lids or cellophane and label the jars.

Opposite: *Redcurrant, Raspberry and Rose Jam (page 53), Melon, Strawberry and Lime Jam (page 44) and Tomato, Lemon and Ginger Jam (page 66)*

Pineapple and Tomato Jam with Lemon and Cinnamon

A deep orange jam, speckled with red. Its faintly oriental spicy taste is sensational with drop scones and fruit buns or bread.

makes 1 kg/2¼ lb/2 jars

1 medium pineapple, about 900 g/2 lb, peeled and with eyes removed
350 g/12 oz ripe tomatoes
30 ml/2 tbsp lemon juice
5 cm/2 in piece of cinnamon stick
700 g/1½ lb/3 cups jam sugar

1 Slice the pineapple, then cut the slices into chunks. Cut each tomato into eighths. Coarsely grind both together in food processor.

2 Put into 4 litre/7 pt/17½ cup capacity bowl, leave uncovered and cook on Full (750–800w) for 10 minutes, stirring twice with a wooden spoon.

3 Add all the remaining ingredients. Leave uncovered and cook on Full for 10 minutes until the sugar has dissolved, stirring twice.

4 Reduce the power to Medium (550w) and continue to cook for a further 25–30 minutes until setting point is reached, stirring three or four times.

5 Allow to cool to lukewarm, then ladle into warmed jars, top with paper discs and leave until cold.

6 Cover with lids or cellophane and label the jars.

Opposite: *Lavender and Rosemary Apple Jelly (page 77)*

Dark Plum and Banana Jam

Banana is not often used in preserves, but in this recipe it makes a dark and dramatic jam, sensually spiced with cardamom.

makes 1.25 kg/2½ lb/2 large jars

700 g/1½ lb dark red plums, halved and stoned (pitted)
1 large or 2 small bananas, about 225 g/8 oz, peeled and sliced
15 ml/1 tbsp lemon juice
Dark seeds from 4 green cardamom pods
150 ml/¼ pt/⅔ cup boiling water
700 g/1½ lb/3 cups granulated sugar

1 Put the plums, banana slices, lemon juice and cardamom seeds in a 4 litre/7 pt/ 17½ cup capacity bowl and add the boiling water. Cover and cook on Full (750–800w) for 15 minutes, stirring once.

2 Uncover, mash the fruit down with a potato masher and stir in the sugar.

3 Cook on Full for 8 minutes until the sugar has dissolved, stirring twice with a wooden spoon.

4 Reduce the power to Medium (550w) and continue to cook for 30 minutes until setting point is reached, stirring three or four times.

5 Allow to cool to lukewarm, then ladle into warmed jars, top with paper discs and leave until cold.

6 Cover with lids or cellophane and label the jars.

Raspberry Jam

An exquisitely scented jam, best made in small quantities.

makes 700 g/1½ lb/2 small jars

> 450 g/1 lb/2 cups granulated sugar
> 450 g/1 lb raspberries

1 Tip the sugar into a 3 litre/5 pt/12½ cup capacity bowl. Crush the raspberries and add to the sugar, combining well. Cover and leave to stand for 1 hour.

2 Uncover and cook on Full (750–800w) for 5 minutes.

3 Stir well with a wooden spoon, then reduce the power to Medium (550w) and continue to cook uncovered for about 25 minutes until setting point is reached, stirring three times with a wooden spoon.

4 Allow to cool to lukewarm, then ladle into warmed jars, top with paper discs and leave until cold.

5 Cover with lids or cellophane and label the jars.

Frozen Raspberry Jam

makes 700 g/1½ lb/2 small jars

As raspberries freeze well, they are one of the few soft fruits available in the shops all year round, and they convert successfully into fine-flavoured, brightly coloured jam. Prepare as for Raspberry Jam, but substitute frozen raspberries for fresh and jam sugar for granulated sugar.

Frozen Summer Fruit Jam

makes 700 g/1½ lb/2 small jars

Prepare as for Frozen Raspberry Jam, but use packs of frozen summer fruits consisting of raspberries, blackcurrants, redcurrants, blackberries and perhaps cherries. After leaving the sugar and fruit to stand, stir in 75 ml/5 tbsp boiling water before starting to microwave.

Minted Redcurrant and Rhubarb Jam

A tantalising jam that can also be used as a condiment to serve with roast lamb and goose.

makes 900 g/2 lb/2 jars

450 g/1 lb redcurrants, stalks removed

250 g/9 oz rhubarb, trimmed and cut into chunks

12 small mint leaves

30 ml/2 tbsp lemon juice

150 ml/¹/₄ pt/²/₃ cup boiling water

700 g/1¹/₂ lb/3 cups jam sugar

1 Put the redcurrants, rhubarb, mint leaves and lemon juice in a 4 litre/7 pt/17¹/₂ cup capacity bowl and add the boiling water. Cover and cook on Full (750–800w) for 12 minutes, stirring once.

2 Uncover, stir in the sugar and cook on Full for 8 minutes until the sugar has dissolved, stirring twice with a wooden spoon.

3 Reduce the power to Medium (550w) and continue to cook for 25 minutes until setting point is reached, stirring three or four times.

4 Allow to cool to lukewarm, then ladle into warmed jars, top with paper discs and leave until cold.

5 Cover with lids or cellophane and label the jars.

Redcurrant, Raspberry and Rose Jam

A dazzler of a bright red jam tinted with rose. See photograph opposite page 48.

makes 1.25 kg/2½ lb/2 large jars

225 g/8 oz redcurrants, stalks removed
90 ml/6 tbsp boiling water
450 g/1 lb raspberries
700 g/1½ lb/3 cups granulated sugar
30 ml/2 tbsp rose water

1 Put the redcurrants in a 4 litre/7 pt/17½ cup capacity bowl and add the boiling water. Cover and cook on Full (750–800w) for 6 minutes, stirring once.

2 Uncover, crush in the raspberries and stir in the sugar.

3 Cook on Full for 7 minutes until the sugar has dissolved, stirring twice with a wooden spoon.

4 Reduce the power to Medium (550w) and continue to cook for 20–25 minutes until setting point is reached, stirring three or four times.

5 Stir in the rose water.

6 Allow to cool to lukewarm, then ladle into warmed jars, top with paper discs and leave until cold.

7 Cover with lids or cellophane and label the jars.

Summer Fruit Jam with Port

A dark, dramatic jam, which is perfect for gifts.

makes 1.5 kg/3 lb/3 jars

225 g/8 oz strawberries, hulled and sliced

225 g/8 oz redcurrants, stalks removed

225 g/8 oz blackberries

200 g/7 oz blueberries

300 ml/$\frac{1}{2}$ pt/1$\frac{1}{4}$ cups port

10 ml/2 tsp finely grated (shredded) rind from any loose-skinned citrus fruit

1 kg/2$\frac{1}{4}$ lb/4$\frac{1}{2}$ cups jam sugar

1 Put all the ingredients except the sugar in a 4 litre/7 pt/17$\frac{1}{2}$ cup capacity bowl. Cover and cook on Full (750–800w) for 13 minutes, stirring once.

2 Stir in the sugar and cook on Full for 8 minutes until the sugar has dissolved, stirring twice with a wooden spoon.

3 Reduce the power to Medium (550w) and continue to cook for 25–30 minutes until setting point is reached, stirring three or four times.

4 Allow to cool to lukewarm, then ladle into warmed jars, top with paper discs and leave until cold.

5 Cover with lids or cellophane and label the jars.

Rhubarb and Ginger Jam

Fresh ginger combined with rhubarb makes a fragrant and tangy jam with a softish set.

makes 1.25 kg/2½ lb/2 large jars

900 g/2 lb rhubarb, trimmed and cut into 2.5 cm/1 in chunks
2 walnut-sized knobs of fresh root ginger, thinly peeled and chopped
30 ml/2 tbsp lemon juice
700 g/1½ lb/3 cups jam sugar

1 Place the rhubarb in a 4 litre/7 pt/17½ cup capacity bowl. Add the ginger and lemon juice.

2 Cover with a plate or lid and cook on Medium (550w) for about 12–14 minutes until soft and pulpy, stirring once.

3 Uncover and stir in the sugar, then cook on Full (750–800w) for 7 minutes until the sugar has dissolved, stirring three times with a wooden spoon.

4 Reduce the power to Medium and continue to cook for about 30 minutes until setting point is reached, stirring three or four times.

5 Allow to cool to lukewarm, then ladle into warmed jars, top with paper discs and leave until cold.

6 Cover with lids or cellophane and label the jars.

Rhubarb, Lavender and Lemon Jam

A refreshing, soft-set and orangey-pink jam, intriguingly scented with lavender and lemon.

makes 1 kg/2¼ lb/2 jars

750 g/1¾ lb rhubarb, trimmed and cut into chunks
4 clusters of lavender flowers, rinsed
2.5 ml/½ tsp grated (shredded) lemon rind
Juice of 1½ large lemons
90 ml/6 tbsp boiling water
700 g/1½ lb/3 cups jam sugar

1 Put the rhubarb, lavender flowers, lemon rind and lemon juice in a 4 litre/7 pt/ 17½ cup capacity bowl and add the boiling water. Cover and cook on Full (750–800w) for 12 minutes, stirring once.

2 Uncover, stir in the sugar and cook on Full for 8 minutes until the sugar has dissolved, stirring twice with a wooden spoon.

3 Reduce the power to Medium (550w) and continue to cook for 30–35 minutes until setting point is reached, stirring three or four times.

4 Allow to cool to lukewarm, then ladle into warmed jars, top with paper discs and leave until cold.

5 Cover with lids or cellophane and label the jars.

Strawberry Jam

Because whole strawberries don't take too well to microwave treatment, I have used sliced fruit instead, which gives perfect results.

makes 1.25 kg/2½ lb/2 large jars

700 g/1½ lb strawberries, hulled and sliced
725 g/1 lb 10 oz/3¼ cups jam sugar

1 Put the fruit and sugar in a 4 litre/7 pt/17½ cup capacity bowl. Stir well, cover and leave to stand for 1 hour.

2 Half-cover and warm through on Full (750–800w) for 8 minutes.

3 Uncover, reduce the power to Medium (550w) and continue to cook for about 20–25 minutes until setting point is reached, stirring three times with a wooden spoon.

4 Allow to cool to lukewarm, then ladle into warmed jars, top with paper discs and leave until cold.

5 Cover with lids or cellophane and label the jars.

Strawberry and Pineapple Jam with Cointreau

A show-stopper, full of charm and based on a combination of fruits that came from the Russian repertoire of classic cooking.

makes 1.5 kg/3 lb/3 jars

1 medium pineapple, about 900 g/2 lb prepared weight, peeled and with eyes removed
450 g/1 lb strawberries, washed, hulled and thinly sliced
I kg/2¼ lb/4½ cups jam sugar
30 ml/2 tbsp Cointreau

1 Slice the pineapple, then cut each slice into chunks. Grind coarsely in a food processor.

2 Place the pineapple in a 4 litre/7 pt/17½ cup capacity bowl and add the strawberries. Leave uncovered and cook on Full (750–800w) for 8 minutes.

3 Stir in the sugar, then cook on Full for a further 7 minutes until the sugar has dissolved, stirring twice with a wooden spoon.

4 Reduce the power to Medium (550w) and cook for about 25 minutes until setting point is reached, stirring three or four times.

5 Stir in the Cointreau and continue to cook on Medium for a further 3 minutes.

6 Allow to cool to lukewarm, then ladle into warmed jars, top with paper discs and leave until cold.

7 Cover with lids or cellophane and label the jars.

Strawberry and Star Fruit Jam with Grenadine

A flotilla of fruits makes for a jam with a pretty colour and charming flavour. The yellow star fruit, or carambola, is native to Asia and when sliced resembles a five-pointed star. Grenadine is a light red syrup made from pomegranates and is used in drinks and desserts.

makes 1 kg/2¼ lb/2 jars

450 g/1 lb strawberries, hulled and sliced
3 star fruit, about 350 g/12 oz, ridges thinly pared and fruit sliced
30 ml/2 tbsp lemon juice
60 ml/4 tbsp grenadine
750 g/1¾ lb/3½ cups jam sugar

1 Put the strawberries, star fruit, lemon juice and grenadine in a 4 litre/7 pt/17½ cup capacity bowl. Cover and cook on Full (750–800w) for 15 minutes, stirring once.

2 Uncover, stir in the sugar and cook on Full for a further 8 minutes until the sugar has dissolved, stirring twice with a wooden spoon.

3 Reduce the power to Medium (550w) and continue to cook for a further 25–30 minutes until setting point is reached, stirring three or four times.

4 Allow to cool to lukewarm, then ladle into warmed jars, top with paper discs and leave until cold.

5 Cover with lids or cellophane and label the jars.

Strawberry and Papaya Jam

The combination of tropical papaya with very British strawberries produces a lovely, delicate balance of flavour and colour. Papayas, also known as paw paws, are native to tropical America and are said to taste like a blend of strawberries, peaches and red rose petals.

makes 1.5 kg/3 lb/3 jars

1 very large or 3 medium just-ripe papayas, about 900 g/2 lb
450 g/1 lb strawberries, hulled and sliced
Juice of 1 large lemon
1 kg/2¼ lb/4½ cups jam sugar

1 Peel and halve the papayas, then remove and discard the inside black seeds with a spoon. Cut the flesh into small cubes and place in a 4 litre/7 pt/17½ cup capacity bowl with the strawberries and lemon juice.

2 Cover and cook on Full (750–800w) for 15 minutes, stirring once.

3 Uncover and stir in the sugar. Cook on Full for 8 minutes until the sugar has dissolved, stirring twice with a wooden spoon.

4 Reduce the power to Medium (500w) and continue to cook for a further 25–30 minutes until setting point is reached, stirring three or four times.

5 Allow to cool to lukewarm, then ladle into warmed jars, top with paper discs and leave until cold.

6 Cover with lids or cellophane and label the jars.

Strawberry and Apricot Jam with Orange

A gloriously vibrant summer jam, unusually highlighted with orange.

makes 1.5 kg/3 lb/3 jars

450 g/1 lb strawberries, hulled and sliced
500 g/18 oz apricots, halved, stoned (pitted) and thinly sliced
Finely grated (shredded) rind and juice of 1 medium orange
900 g/2 lb/4 cups jam sugar

1 Put the strawberries, apricots, orange rind and juice in a 4 litre/7 pt/17½ cup capacity bowl. Cover and cook on Full (750–800w) for 15 minutes, stirring once.

2 Uncover, stir in the sugar and cook on Full for 8 minutes until the sugar has dissolved, stirring twice with a wooden spoon.

3 Reduce the power to Medium (550w) and continue to cook for a further 25–30 minutes until setting point is reached, stirring three or four times.

4 Allow to cool to lukewarm, then ladle into warmed jars, top with paper discs and leave until cold.

5 Cover with lids or cellophane and label the jars.

Strawberry and Mixed Currant Jam with Melon and Gin

Gin adds a magical touch of juniper to the jam, flavouring it with the utmost discretion.

makes 1.5 kg/3 lb/3 jars

450 g/1 lb strawberries, hulled and sliced
350 g/12 oz mixed redcurrants and blackcurrants, stalks removed
350 g/12 oz honeydew or ogen melon, peeled, seeded and cubed
900 g/2 lb/4 cups jam sugar
30 ml/2 tbsp gin

1 Place the strawberries, redcurrants, blackcurrants and melon in a 4 litre/7 pt/17½ cup capacity bowl. Cover and cook on Full (750–800w) for 10 minutes, stirring once.

2 Uncover, stir in the sugar and cook on Full for 8 minutes until the sugar has dissolved, stirring once with a wooden spoon.

3 Reduce the power to Medium (550w) and continue to cook for 30–35 minutes until setting point is reached, stirring three or four times.

4 Stir in the gin.

5 Allow to cool to lukewarm, then ladle into warmed jars, top with paper discs and leave until cold.

6 Cover with lids or cellophane and label the jars.

Strawberry, Ginger and Rose Jam

An exquisitely and exotically scented jam with a wonderful rosy colouring.

makes 700 g/1½ lb/2 small jars

450 g/1 lb strawberries, hulled and sliced
450 g/1 lb/2 cups jam sugar
30 ml/2 tbsp ginger cordial
30 ml/2 tbsp rose water

1 Put the strawberries in a 3 litre/5 pt/12½ cup capacity bowl, cover and cook on Full (750–800w) for 7 minutes.

2 Mash down the strawberries with a fork, then stir in the sugar, ginger cordial and rose water. Cook on Full for 8 minutes until the sugar has dissolved, stirring twice with a wooden spoon.

3 Reduce the power to Medium (550w) and continue to cook for 20–25 minutes until setting point is reached, stirring three or four times.

4 Allow to cool to lukewarm, then ladle into warmed jars, top with paper discs and leave until cold.

5 Cover with lids or cellophane and label the jars.

Strawberry and Fresh Fig Jam

An unlikely sounding combination that actually works superbly.

makes 1.5 kg/3 lb/3 jars

> 450 g/1 lb strawberries, hulled and sliced
> 450 g/1 lb fleshy figs, hulled and coarsely chopped
> 45 ml/3 tbsp lemon juice
> 45 ml/3 tbsp boiling water
> 1 kg/2¼ lb/4½ cups jam sugar

1 Put the strawberries, figs and lemon juice in a 4 litre/7 pt/17½ cup capacity bowl and add the boiling water. Cover and cook on Full (750–800w) for 7 minutes, stirring once.

2 Uncover, stir in the sugar and cook on Full for 10 minutes until the sugar has dissolved, stirring twice with a wooden spoon.

3 Reduce the power to Medium (550w) and continue to cook for 25–30 minutes until setting point is reached, stirring three or four times.

4 Allow to cool to lukewarm, then ladle into warmed jars, top with paper discs and leave until cold.

5 Cover with lids or cellophane and label the jars.

Tamarillo and Apple Jam

Tamarillos come mostly from South America and New Zealand and taste like a cross between tomato and physalis. They are close to Italian plum tomatoes in outward appearance although the skin is more orange than red, the flesh below is golden and the seeded centres are purple. They have a novelty appeal and are a pert combination with apple in this jam.

makes 1.6 kg/3½ lb/3 large jars

> 700 g/1½ lb tamarillos, about 7 fruit, coarsely chopped
> 500 g/18 oz cooking (tart) apples, peeled, cored and coarsely chopped
> 150 ml/¼ pt/⅔ cup boiling water
> 1 kg/2¼ lb/4½ cups granulated sugar

1 Put the tamarillos and apples in a 4 litre/7 pt/17½ cup capacity bowl and add the boiling water. Cover and cook on Full (750–800w) for 15 minutes, stirring twice.

2 Uncover, stir in the sugar and cook on Full for 8 minutes until the sugar has dissolved, stirring twice.

3 Reduce the power to Medium (550w) and continue to cook for 25–30 minutes until setting point is reached, stirring three or four times.

4 Allow to cool to lukewarm, then ladle into warmed jars, top with paper discs and leave until cold.

5 Cover with lids or cellophane and label the jars.

Tomato, Lemon and Ginger Jam

Borrowed from North America and South Africa where tomato jam is popular and less eccentric than one might imagine. This is a seriously good jam and well worth trying. See photograph opposite page 48.

makes 1.25 kg/2½ lb/2 large jars

700 g/1½ lb tomatoes, skinned and chopped
Finely grated (shredded) rind and juice of 2 large lemons
7.5 ml/1½ tsp ground ginger
700 g/1½ lb/3 cups granulated sugar

1 Put the tomatoes, lemon rind and juice in a 4 litre/7 pt/17½ cup capacity bowl and stir in the ginger. Leave uncovered and cook on Full (750–800w) for 10 minutes, stirring once.

2 Stir in the sugar and cook on Full for 8 minutes until the sugar has dissolved, stirring twice with a wooden spoon.

3 Reduce the power to Medium (550w) and continue to cook for 20–25 minutes until setting point is reached, stirring three or four times.

4 Allow to cool to lukewarm, then ladle into warmed jars, top with paper discs and leave until cold.

5 Cover with lids or cellophane and label the jars.

Marmalades

Don't restrict yourself to the **traditional** orange marmalade: try this selection of superb marmalades made with a wide **range** of ingredients. Since you are only making one or two pots at a time, you can afford to have a different **marmalade** for every day of the week!

Seville Orange Marmalade

The most superior marmalade of all with a vibrant flavour and bright orange colour. See photograph opposite page 72.

makes 1.6 kg/3½ lb/3 large jars

700 g/1½ lb Seville (bitter) oranges
1.25 litres/2 pts/5 cups boiling water
1.25 kg/2½ lb/5 cups granulated sugar

1 Quarter the oranges and place the pips in a square of muslin (cheesecloth) or a coffee filter bag. Tie the pips securely in the bag. Slice the orange quarters thinly.

2 Put the fruit in a 4 litre/7 pt/17½ cup capacity bowl with the bag of pips, then stir in the boiling water. Cover and leave to soak for 3 hours.

3 Still covered, cook on Medium (550w) for 30 minutes, stirring three or four times.

4 Uncover, stir in the sugar and cook on Full (750–800w) for 10 minutes until the sugar has dissolved, stirring twice with a wooden spoon.

5 Reduce the power to Medium and continue to cook for 45 minutes until setting point is reached, stirring four or five times.

6 Remove the bag of pips.

7 Allow to cool to lukewarm, then ladle into warmed jars, top with paper discs and leave until cold.

8 Cover with lids or cellophane and label the jars.

Marmalades should be stored in a cool, dark place and can be kept for up to a year but must be checked regularly for mildew at two-month intervals.

Chunky Orange and Mango Marmalade

The curious combination of orange and mango is surprising for a marmalade but comes off brilliantly.

makes 1.6 kg/3½ lb/3 large jars

450 g/1 lb sweet oranges
2 medium, slightly under-ripe mangoes, about 450 g/1 lb
900 ml/1½ pts/3¾ cups boiling water
1 kg/2¼ lb/4½ cups jam sugar

1 Slice the oranges thinly, discarding the pips. Peel the mangoes thinly, then cut slices of flesh away from the centre stones (pits). Put the oranges and mangoes in a food processor and coarsely chop. Transfer to a 4 litre/7pt/17½ cup capacity bowl. Mix in the boiling water, then cover and leave to soak for 3 hours.

2 Still covered, cook on Medium (550w) for 30 minutes.

3 Stir in the sugar and cook, uncovered, on Full (750–800w) for 10 minutes until the sugar has dissolved, stirring twice with a wooden spoon.

4 Continue to cook on Medium for 25–30 minutes until setting point is reached, stirring three or four times.

5 Allow to cool to lukewarm, then ladle into warmed jars, top with paper discs and leave until cold.

6 Cover with lids or cellophane and label the jars.

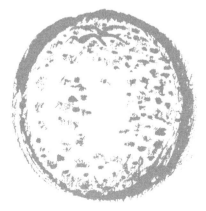

Canned Fruit Marmalade

The easy way to great marmalade – using ready-prepared, canned fruit. It produces a trouble-free marmalade with a firm set and predictable flavour. Quite basic but very tasty and useful.

makes 1.5 kg/3 lb/3 jars

> 425 g/15 oz/2 cups canned prepared lemons or oranges
> 250 ml/8 fl oz/1 cup boiling water
> 900 g/2 lb/4 cups granulated sugar

1 Put the fruit in a 4 litre/7 pt/17½ cup capacity bowl and stir in the boiling water. Cook, uncovered, on Full (750–800w) for 10 minutes, stirring twice.

2 Stir in the sugar and continue to cook on Full for a further 9 minutes until the sugar has dissolved, stirring twice with a wooden spoon.

3 Reduce the power to Medium (550w) and continue to cook for 20–30 minutes until setting point is reached, stirring three or four times. The mixture rises in the bowl fairly quickly while cooking and needs careful watching to prevent spillage. The best thing to do is to open and shut the microwave door if you think the marmalade is about to boil over.

4 Allow to cool to lukewarm, then ladle into warmed jars, top with paper discs and leave until cold.

5 Cover with lids or cellophane and label the jars.

Oxford-style Four-fruit Marmalade

A dramatically dark and richly fruited marmalade, coloured with black treacle (molasses). Leaving the marmalade to stand until lukewarm before potting it ensures that the citrus peel remains evenly distributed.

makes 1.6 kg/3¹/₂ lb/3 large jars

550 g/1¹/₄ lb mixed citrus fruits to include: 1 lime, 1 medium yellow grapefruit, 1 small orange, 1 small thin-skinned lemon
900 ml/1¹/₂ pts/3³/₄ cups boiling water
1 kg/2¹/₄ lb/4¹/₂ cups granulated sugar
15–30 ml/1–2 tbsp black treacle (molasses)

1 Quarter all the fruits and place the pips in a square of muslin (cheesecloth) or a coffee filter bag. Tie the pips securely in the bag. Slice the fruit thinly.

2 Put the fruit in a 4 litre/7 pt/17¹/₂ cup capacity bowl with the bag of pips, then stir in the boiling water. Cover and leave to soak for 3 hours.

3 Still covered, cook on Medium (550w) for 30 minutes, stirring four times.

4 Uncover, stir in the sugar and treacle and cook on Full (750–800w) for 10 minutes until the sugar has dissolved, stirring twice with a wooden spoon.

5 Reduce the power to Medium and continue to cook for 25–30 minutes until setting point is reached, stirring three or four times. Remove the bag of pips.

6 Allow to cool to lukewarm, then ladle into warmed jars, top with paper discs and leave until cold.

7 Cover with lids or cellophane and label the jars.

Whisky Marmalade

makes 1.6 kg/3¹/₂ lb/3 large jars

Prepare as for Oxford-style Four-fruit Marmalade, but stir in 15–30 ml/1–2 tbsp whisky when the marmalade has reached setting point.

Thick-cut Kumquat and Lemon Marmalade

Bursting with magical citrus aromas, this is a zippy marmalade with a sparkling personality.

makes 1.2 kg/2½ lb/2 large jars

400 g/14 oz kumquats
1 large lemon, about 75 g/3 oz
1 litre/1¾ pts/4¼ cups boiling water
1 kg/2¼ lb/4½ cups jam sugar

1 Arrange the kumquats in a single layer on a large plate. Leave uncovered and cook on Medium (550w) for 3 minutes. Rinse the fruit and wipe it dry, then slice thinly, saving the pips.

2 Cook the lemon on Defrost, Simmer or Medium-low (270–300w) for 3 minutes. Grate (shred) the peel and squeeze out the juice, saving the pips and pith. Cut up the pith and tie in a clean piece of muslin (cheesecloth) with the kumquat pips and lemon pips.

3 Put the kumquat slices, lemon peel and juice and the bag of pips and pith in a 4 litre/7 pt/17½ cup capacity bowl and add the boiling water. Cover and leave to soak for a minimum of 12 hours.

4 Still covered, cook on Medium (550w) for 30 minutes, stirring three times.

5 Uncover, stir in the sugar and cook on Full (750–800w) for 10 minutes until the sugar has dissolved, stirring twice with a wooden spoon.

6 Reduce the power to Medium and continue to cook for 25–30 minutes until setting point is reached, stirring three or four times. Remove the bag of pips and pith.

7 Allow to cool to lukewarm, then ladle into warmed jars, top with paper discs and leave until cold.

8 Cover with lids or cellophane and label the jars.

Opposite: *Seville Orange Marmalade (page 68)*

Pineapple and Orange Marmalade

The combination of pineapple and orange in this marmalade is almost magical. The colour is a mellow yellow and the set firm and reliable. One of the best.

makes 1 kg/2¼ lb/2 large jars

1 medium–large pineapple, about 900 g/2 lb, peeled and with eyes removed
1 large orange, about 350 g/12 oz, coarsely chopped
900 g/2 lb/4 cups jam sugar

1 Slice the pineapple thickly, then cut each slice into chunks. Grind to a coarse purée (paste) with the orange in a food processor.

2 Put in a 4 litre/7 pt/17½ cup capacity bowl. Stir in the sugar and leave to stand for 1 hour.

3 Leave uncovered and cook on Full (750–800w) for 10 minutes until the sugar has dissolved, stirring three times with a wooden spoon.

4 Reduce the power to Medium (550w) and continue to cook for a further 30–35 minutes until setting point is reached, stirring three or four times.

5 Allow to cool to lukewarm, then ladle into warmed jars, top with paper discs and leave until cold.

6 Cover with lids or cellophane and label the jars.

Opposite: *Fat-free Fresh Grape Mincemeat (page 104)*

Clear Lemon and Lime Jelly Marmalade

This jellied marmalade is ideal for those who like clear, typically bitter-sweet marmalade. It needs more preparation than most of the others but it's worth the effort. Reserve the pulp to make Indian-style Hot Lime Chutney Pickle (see page 149).

makes 1.7 kg/3¾ lb/3 large jars

> 450 g/1 lb limes
> 450 g/1 lb lemons
> 1.5 litres/2½ pts/6 cups boiling water
> 900 g/2 lb/4 cups granulated sugar

1 Arrange the limes and lemons in a single layer on a plate and cook on Medium (550w) for 2 minutes. Cut into small chunks, then grind, with the pips, fairly finely in a food processor.

2 Transfer to a 4 litre/7 pt/17½ cup capacity bowl and add 1.2 litres/2 pts/5 cups of the boiling water. Cover and leave to soak for 1 hour.

3 Uncover and cook on Full (750–800w) for 10 minutes, stirring twice. Cover and cook on Medium for 25 minutes.

4 Stir in the remaining boiling water. Pour the fruit and liquid carefully into a fine muslin (cheesecloth) jelly bag or fine nylon sieve (strainer) suspended over a bowl. Leave to drip for 12 hours, stirring the mixture round with a spoon periodically for the first 2 hours.

5 Pour the liquid into a measuring jug and make up to 1.2 litres/2 pts/5 cups with cold water, if necessary. Transfer to a bowl and cook on Full for 10 minutes, stirring once.

6 Stir in the sugar and cook on Full for 10 minutes until it has dissolved, stirring twice with a wooden spoon.

7 Reduce the power to Medium and continue to cook for 20–25 minutes until setting point is reached, stirring three or four times.

8 Allow to cool to lukewarm, then ladle into warmed jars, top with paper discs and leave until cold.

9 Cover with lids or cellophane and label the jars.

Jellies

With their jewel-like sparkle, mellow colours, brilliant clarity and fine flavours, jellies are the classic sophisticates of the preserve family, equally at home as condiments with savouries, spread on toast or teabreads, or used for glazing sweet confections and also for holding trimmings in place on cakes.

Apple Jelly

A delicate, all-purpose jelly. As whole pieces of fruit are used, windfalls are perfect, provided bruised parts are cut away and the weight required is maintained by adding extra fruit if necessary (see pages 9–10).

makes 1.25 kg/2½ lb/2 large jars

1.5 kg/3 lb cooking (tart) apples
1.2 litres/2 pts/5 cups boiling water
700 g/1½ lb/3 cups granulated sugar

1 Wash the apples well, then cut them into smallish chunks without peeling or coring. Put in a 4 litre/7 pt/17½ cup bowl and add the boiling water.

2 Leave uncovered and cook on Full (750–800w) for 15–20 minutes until the apples are soft and very pulpy, stirring three times with a wooden spoon.

3 Break down the apples with a potato masher and leave until cold.

4 Tip the apples and their liquid carefully into a large jelly bag or nylon sieve (strainer) suspended over a large mixing bowl and leave to drip for 12–14 hours. You can help it on its way initially by stirring the contents gently round in the bag a few times and even giving the bag an occasional light squeeze to release the juice. Do not exert too much pressure as small fragments of pulp may get through the bag and cloud the jelly.

5 Pour the juices into a measuring jug and make up to 900 ml/1½ pts/3¾ cups with cold water if necessary. (The quantity will depend on the juiciness of the fruit.)

6 Return to the original bowl, leave uncovered and heat on Full for 10 minutes.

7 Stir in the sugar and cook on Full for a further 10 minutes until the sugar has dissolved, stirring three or four times.

8 Reduce the power to Medium (550w) and continue to cook for 25–30 minutes until setting point is reached, stirring three or four times.

9 Allow to cool to lukewarm, then ladle into warmed jars, top with paper discs and leave until cold. Cover with lids or cellophane and label the jars.

Minted Apple Jelly

makes 1.25 kg/2¹⁄₂ lb/2 large jars

Prepare as for Apple Jelly, but when the jelly is just beginning to settle and set in the jars, gently stir in a few small mint leaves.

Pink Apple Jelly

makes 1.25 kg/2¹⁄₂ lb/2 large jars

Prepare as for Apple Jelly, but just after adding the sugar, add 30 ml/2 tbsp crème de mûre (blackberry liqueur) or crème de cassis (blackcurrant liqueur).

Rosemary Apple Jelly

makes 1.25 kg/2¹⁄₂ lb/2 large jars

Prepare as for Apple Jelly, but when the jelly is just beginning to settle and set in the jars, gently push into each jar one or two sprigs of fresh rosemary. See photograph opposite page 49.

Lavender Apple Jelly

makes 1.25 kg/2¹⁄₂ lb/2 large jars

Prepare as for Apple Jelly, but when the jelly is just beginning to settle and set in the jars, gently push into each jar some stems of fresh lavender flowers with a few leaves also still attached. See photograph opposite page 49.

Provided jellies are stored in a cool, dark and dry place, their shelf life is as long as jam, but you must check at two-month intervals for any mildew and discard the jelly if you find any.

Bakers' Apricot Jelly

This clear jelly is a treat to have in the kitchen but is not readily found in shops. It can be used as a spread to glaze cakes and pastries and is a preserve preferred by top chefs for high-class patisserie and desserts. It is also fairly economical to make. The leftover fruit becomes almost glacéed and is luxurious eaten with cream and can also be used to decorate the tops of cakes and puddings.

makes 1.25 kg/2½ lb/2 large jars

225 g/8 oz dried apricots, cut into pieces
600 ml/1 pt/2¼ cups cold water
300 ml/½ pt/1¼ cups boiling water
60 ml/4 tbsp lemon juice
900 g/2 lb/4 cups jam sugar

1 Put the apricots and cold water in a 4 pt/7 litre/17½ cup capacity bowl. Leave uncovered and cook on Full (750–800w) for 10 minutes. Leave to stand for 2 hours to give the fruit time to absorb some of the liquid and swell.

2 Add the boiling water, cover and cook on Full for 15 minutes.

3 Uncover, stir in the lemon juice and sugar and cook on Full for 10 minutes, stirring three or four times with a wooden spoon until the sugar has dissolved.

4 Reduce the power to Medium (550w) and cook for 25–30 minutes until setting point is reached, stirring three or four times.

5 Allow to cool slightly. Strain carefully through a fine nylon or mesh sieve (strainer) into a large bowl. Ladle into warmed jars, top with paper discs and leave until cold. Cover with lids or cellophane and label the jars.

Dried Fruit Salad Jelly

makes 1.25 kg/2½ lb/2 large jars

Prepare as for Bakers' Apricot Jelly, but use dried mixed fruit salad instead of apricots. Snip the fruit with scissors and remove any prune stones (pits) after the fruit has been standing for 2 hours.

Blackberry Jelly

If you have the opportunity of going blackberrying in the autumn (fall), gather some extra berries for this superior jelly with its unique taste of woodland Britain.

makes 750 g/1¾ lb/2 small jars

700 g/1½ lb freshly picked blackberries
600 ml/1 pt/2½ cups boiling water
450 g/1 lb/2 cups jam sugar

1 Put the blackberries in a 3 litre/5 pt/12½ cup capacity bowl and add the boiling water. Leave uncovered and cook on Full (750–800w) for 12 minutes until the fruit is soft and pulpy.

2 Break down the fruit with a potato masher and leave until cold.

3 Carefully tip the fruit and liquid into a large jelly bag or nylon sieve (strainer) suspended over a large mixing bowl and leave to drip for 12–14 hours. You can help it on its way initially by stirring the contents gently round in the bag with a spoon a few times and even giving the bag an occasional light squeeze to release the juice. Do not exert too much pressure as small fragments of pulp may get through the bag and cloud the jelly.

4 Pour the juices into a measuring jug and make up to 600 ml/1 pt/2½ cups with cold water if necessary.

5 Return to the original bowl, leave uncovered and cook on Full for 10 minutes.

6 Stir in the sugar and cook on Full for a further 10 minutes until the sugar has dissolved, stirring three or four times with a wooden spoon.

7 Reduce the power to Medium (550w) and cook for 25–30 minutes until setting point is reached, stirring three or four times.

8 Allow to cool to lukewarm, then ladle into warmed jars, top with paper discs and leave until cold. Cover with lids or cellophane and label the jars.

Cranberry Jelly

The prettiest of golden-pink jellies, this is the natural companion to chicken and turkey, or even Swedish-style fried (sautéed) meat balls. If fresh berries are out of season, use berries straight from frozen. You could add the finely grated (shredded) rind of two clementines with the sugar for extra flavour.

makes 900 g/2 lb/2 jars

700 g/1½ lb cranberries
900 ml/1½ pts/3¾ cups boiling water
15 ml/1 tbsp lemon juice
550 g/1¼ lb/2½ cups jam sugar

1 Put the cranberries in a 4 litre/7 pt/17½ cup capacity bowl and add the boiling water. Leave uncovered and cook on Full (750–800w) for 15–20 minutes until the cranberries are soft and very pulpy, stirring two or three times.

2 Break down the fruit with a potato masher and leave until cold.

3 Tip the fruit and liquid carefully into a large jelly bag or fine nylon sieve (strainer) suspended over a large mixing bowl and leave to drip for 12–14 hours. You can help it on its way initially by stirring the contents round in the bag with a spoon a few times and even giving the bag an occasional light squeeze to release the juice. Do not exert too much pressure as small fragments of pulp may get through the bag and cloud the jelly.

4 Pour the juices into a measuring jug and make up to 750 ml/1¼ pts/3 cups with cold water if necessary.

5 Return to the original bowl and add the lemon juice. Leave uncovered and heat on Full for 10 minutes.

6 Stir in the sugar and cook on Full for a further 10 minutes until the sugar has dissolved, stirring twice with a wooden spoon.

7 Reduce the power to Medium (550w) and continue to cook for 25–30 minutes until setting point is reached, stirring three or four times.

8 Allow to cool to lukewarm, then ladle into warmed jars, top with paper discs and leave until cold. Cover with lids or cellophane and label the jars.

Damson and Muscat Jelly

A deep royal red in colour, this tangy and striking jelly makes a great accompaniment for poultry and game, roast venison in particular.

makes 1.2 kg/2½ lb/2 large jars

900 g/2 lb damson plums, halved and stoned (pitted)
300 ml/½ pt/1¼ cups muscatel wine
600 ml/1 pt/2½ cups boiling water
700 g/1½ lb/3 cups granulated sugar

1 Put the damsons and wine in a 4 litre/7 pt/17½ cup capacity bowl and add the boiling water. Cover and cook on Full (750–800w) for 15 minutes.

2 Break down the fruit with a potato masher and leave until cold.

3 Carefully tip the fruit and liquid into a large jelly bag or nylon sieve (strainer) suspended over a large mixing bowl and leave to drip for 12–14 hours. You can help it on its way initially by stirring the contents gently round in the bag with a spoon a few times and even giving the bag an occasional light squeeze to release the juice. Do not exert too much pressure as small fragments of pulp may get through the bag and cloud the jelly.

4 Pour the juices into a measuring jug and make up to 900 ml/1½ pts/3 cups with cold water if necessary.

5 Return to the original bowl, leave uncovered and cook on Full for 10 minutes.

6 Stir in the sugar and cook on Full for a further 10 minutes, stirring three or four times with a wooden spoon.

7 Reduce the power to Medium (550w) and continue to cook for 30–35 minutes until setting point is reached, stirring three or four times.

8 Allow to cool to lukewarm, then ladle into warmed jars, top with paper discs and leave until cold. Cover with lids or cellophane and label the jars.

Elderberry and Apple Jelly

With their rather old-fashioned and traditional flavour, elderberry preserves and cordials are becoming popular again and are well worth making.

makes 900 g/2 lb/2 jars

350 g/12 oz elderberries, stalks removed
700 g/1½ lb cooking (tart) apples
900 ml/1½ pts/3¾ cups boiling water
550 g/1¼ lb/2½ cups granulated sugar

1 Put the elderberries in a 4 litre/7 pt/17½ cup capacity bowl. Cut the apples into small pieces without peeling or coring. Add them to the elderberries with the boiling water.

2 Leave uncovered and cook on Full (750–800w) for 13 minutes until the fruits are very soft and pulpy, stirring two or three times.

3 Break down the fruit with a potato masher and leave until cold.

4 Carefully tip the fruit and liquid into a large jelly bag or nylon sieve (strainer) suspended over a large mixing bowl and leave to drip for 12–14 hours. You can help it on its way initially by stirring the contents gently round in the bag with a spoon a few times and even giving the bag an occasional light squeeze to release the juice. Do not exert too much pressure as small fragments of pulp may get through the bag and cloud the jelly.

5 Pour the juices (which will be on the thick side) into a measuring jug and make up to 750 ml/1¼ pts/3 cups with cold water.

6 Transfer to a bowl, leave uncovered and cook on Full for 10 minutes.

7 Stir in the sugar and cook on Full for a further 8 minutes until the sugar has dissolved, stirring three or four times with a wooden spoon.

8 Reduce the power to Medium (550w) and continue to cook for about 35–40 minutes until setting point is reached, stirring three or four times.

9 Allow to cool to lukewarm, then ladle into warmed jars, top with paper discs and leave until cold. Cover with lids or cellophane and label the jars.

Grape Jelly with Apple Juice

Sharpened with cider vinegar and lemon juice, this glistening gold jelly is mild and gentle and goes well with fish and chicken dishes, roast pork, gammon and with crème fraîche on drop scones.

makes 1 kg/2¼ lb/2 large jars

900 g/2 lb seedless green grapes
600 ml/1 pt/2½ cups pure clear apple juice
2–3 whole cloves
60 ml/4 tbsp cider vinegar
30 ml/2 tbsp lemon juice
700 g/1½ lb/3 cups jam sugar

1 Put the grapes, apple juice and cloves in a 4 litre/7 pt/17½ cup capacity bowl. Leave uncovered and cook on Full (750–800w) for 17–18 minutes until soft and pulpy, stirring two or three times.

2 Break down the fruit with a potato masher and leave until cold.

3 Carefully tip the fruit and liquid into a large jelly bag or nylon sieve (strainer) suspended over a large mixing bowl and leave to drip for 12–14 hours. You can help it on its way initially by stirring the contents gently round in the bag with a spoon a few times and even giving the bag an occasional light squeeze to release the juice. Do not exert too much pressure as small fragments of pulp may get through the bag and cloud the jelly.

4 Pour the juices into a measuring jug, add the vinegar and lemon juice, then make up to 900 ml/1½ pts/3¾ cups with cold water if necessary.

5 Transfer to a bowl and cook uncovered on Full for 10 minutes.

6 Stir in the sugar and cook on Full for a further 10 minutes until the sugar has dissolved, stirring three or four times with a wooden spoon.

7 Reduce the power to Medium (550w) and continue to cook for 30–35 minutes until setting point is reached, stirring three or four times.

8 Allow to cool to lukewarm, then ladle into warmed jars, top with paper discs and leave until cold. Cover with non-metallic lids or cellophane and label the jars.

Brandied Red Grape Jelly

A rather grand, festive jelly, cheerfully colourful and warmly flavoured.

makes 1.7 kg/3³⁄₄ lb/3 large jars

1.2 kg/2¹⁄₂ lb black grapes with seeds
3–4 whole cloves
900 ml/1¹⁄₂ pts/3³⁄₄ cups boiling water
700 g/1¹⁄₂ lb/3 cups jam sugar
25 ml/1¹⁄₂ tbsp brandy

1 Put the grapes and cloves in a 4 litre/7 pt/17¹⁄₂ cup capacity bowl and add the boiling water. Leave uncovered and cook on Full (750–800w) for 17–18 minutes until soft and pulpy, stirring two or three times.

2 Break down the fruit with a potato masher and leave until cold.

3 Carefully tip the fruit and liquid into a large jelly bag or nylon sieve (strainer) suspended over a large mixing bowl and leave to drip for 12–14 hours. You can help it on its way initially by stirring the contents gently round in the bag with a spoon a few times and even giving the bag an occasional light squeeze to release the juice. Do not exert too much pressure as small fragments of pulp may get through the bag and cloud the jelly.

4 Pour the juices into a measuring jug and make up to 900 ml/1¹⁄₂ pts/3³⁄₄ cups with cold water if necessary.

5 Return to the original bowl, leave uncovered and cook on Full for 10 minutes.

6 Stir in the sugar and cook on Full for a further 10 minutes until the sugar has dissolved, stirring three or four times with a wooden spoon.

7 Reduce the power to Medium (550w) and continue to cook for 30–35 minutes until setting point is reached, stirring three or four times.

8 Stir in the brandy.

9 Allow to cool to lukewarm, then ladle into warmed jars, top with paper discs and leave until cold. Cover with lids or cellophane and label the jars.

Guava Jelly

Guavas are related to the myrtle and eucalyptus families and are native to tropical America. They look a bit like pears, though the skin tends to be deep yellow and the bouquet of the fruit is strong and unmistakable. When cooked, this unique and special jelly takes on a rose-pink tint and the taste is reminiscent of wild strawberries and honey. It goes particularly well with Greek and Middle Eastern food.

makes 1.2 kg/2¹/₂ lb/2 large jars

700 g/1¹/₂ lb guavas
900 ml/1¹/₂ pts/3¹/₄ cups boiling water
700 g/1¹/₂ lb/3 cups jam sugar

1 Put the guavas in a 4 litre/7 pt/17¹/₂ cup capacity bowl and add the boiling water. Cover with a vented plastic lid and cook on Full (750–800w) for 20 minutes until the fruit is soft and pulpy, stirring two or three times.

2 Break down the fruit with a potato masher and leave until cold.

3 Carefully tip the fruit and liquid into a large jelly bag or nylon sieve (strainer) suspended over a large mixing bowl and leave to drip for 12–14 hours. You can help it on its way initially by stirring the contents gently round in the bag with a spoon a few times and even giving the bag an occasional light squeeze to release the juice. Do not exert too much pressure as small fragments of pulp may get through the bag and cloud the jelly.

4 Pour the juices into a measuring jug and make up to 900 ml/1¹/₂ pt/3¹/₄ cups with cold water if necessary.

5 Return to the original bowl and cook uncovered on Full for 10 minutes.

6 Stir in the sugar and cook on Full for a further 10 minutes until the sugar has dissolved, stirring three or four times with a wooden spoon.

7 Reduce the power to Medium (550w) and cook for 30–35 minutes until setting point is reached, stirring three or four times.

8 Allow to cool to lukewarm, then ladle into warmed jars, top with paper discs and leave until cold. Cover with lids or cellophane and label the jars.

Lemon and Lime Jelly with Apples and Pink Peppercorns

An assertive, refreshing and aromatic jelly cheekily dotted with pink peppercorns. It's outstanding with curries and meaty fish like mackerel. If the peppercorns rise to the tops of the jars, they were added while the jelly was too hot. Stir them gently back into the still warm jelly with a teaspoon so they are evenly distributed.

makes 1.7 kg/3³/₄ lb/3 large jars

> 450 g/1 lb Bramley or other cooking (tart) apples
> 2 unwaxed lemons, about 175 g/6 oz, quartered and thinly sliced
> 2 unwaxed limes, about 100 g/4 oz, quartered and thinly sliced
> 1.2 litres/2 pts/5 cups boiling water
> 1 kg/2¹/₄ lb/4¹/₄ cups golden granulated sugar
> 15 ml/1 tbsp pink peppercorns in brine, well-drained

1 Cut the apples into smallish chunks without peeling or coring. Put in a 4 litre/ 7 pt/17¹/₂ cup capacity bowl with the lemons, limes and boiling water and all the pips. Leave uncovered and cook on Full (750–800w) for 20 minutes until the fruit is soft and pulpy, stirring two or three times. The peel and pith should squash easily when rubbed between finger and thumb.

2 Break down the fruit with a potato masher and leave until cold.

3 Tip the fruit and liquid carefully into a large jelly bag or fine nylon sieve (strainer) suspended over a large mixing bowl and leave to drip for 12–14 hours. You can help it on its way initially by stirring the contents gently round in the bag with a spoon a few times and even giving the bag an occasional light squeeze to release the juice. Do not exert too much pressure as small fragments of pulp may get through the bag and cloud the jelly.

4 Pour the juices into a measuring jug and make up to 1.2 litres/2 pts/5 cups with cold water if necessary. (The quantity will depend on the juiciness of the fruit and the proportion of pith and peel to pulp.)

5 Transfer the juices to a bowl and cook uncovered on Full for 10 minutes.

6 Stir in the sugar and cook on Full for a further 10 minutes until the sugar has dissolved, stirring three or four times with a wooden spoon.

7 Reduce the power to Medium (550w) and continue to cook for 25–30 minutes until setting point is reached, stirring three or four times.

8 Allow to cool to lukewarm, then ladle into warmed jars and leave until the jelly just begins to settle and set.

9 Lightly stir an equal amount of peppercorns into each jar, top with paper discs and leave until cold. Cover with lids or cellophane and label the jars.

Pomegranate Jelly

An eccentric and innovative preserve that goes back to the turn of the twentieth century. This old recipe, adapted for the microwave, produces a delicate and softish, purplish-red jelly with a whimsical flavour and a slight and mysterious hint of beetroot. Eat it with fish and chicken or spoon over rich ice cream or rice pudding.

makes 1 kg/2¼ lb/2 large jars

> 1.75 kg/4 lb/8–12 pomegranates
> 550 g/1¼ lb/2½ cups jam sugar
> 30 ml/2 tbsp lemon juice

1 Halve the pomegranates horizontally. Squeeze out the juice using a lemon squeezer. Line a fine mesh sieve (strainer) with an opened-out coffee filter bag placed over a large jug and pour in the squeezed juice and any bits of fruit that have fallen into it. Leave to drip for 2–3 hours, stirring it round gently from time to time. You should have about 600 ml/1 pt/2½ cups of juice.

2 Pour into a 3 litre/5 pt/12½ cup capacity bowl and add the sugar and half the lemon juice. Cook on Full (750–800w) for 15 minutes until the sugar has dissolved, stirring twice with a wooden spoon.

3 Stir in the remaining lemon juice. Reduce the power to Medium (550w) and cook for 25–30 minutes until setting point is reached, stirring four times.

4 Allow to cool to lukewarm, then ladle into warmed jars, top with paper discs and leave until cold. Cover with lids or cellophane and label the jars.

Luxury Quince Jelly

Those of you with a japonica tree in the garden can have a field day with these deep-yellow skinned and pale-fleshed fruit that turn salmon pink as they cook. Apart from stewed fruit and jam, the fruit converts beautifully into a superb, honey gold and brilliantly clear jelly with a tint of rose and has a unique and unmistakable sweet-sour, almost musty tang.

makes 1.25 kg/2½ lb/2 large jars

1 kg/2¼ lb/2 large quinces
1.2 litres/2 pts/5 cups boiling water
1 kg/2¼ lb/4½ cups jam sugar
15 ml/1 tbsp lemon juice

1 Slice the fruit thickly without peeling or coring. Put in 4 litre/7 pt/17½ cup capacity bowl and add the boiling water. Cover with a large plate or plastic lid and cook on Low (450w) for 45 minutes.

2 Leave to rest for 10 minutes. Uncover and continue to cook on Full (750–800w) for 15–25 minutes until the fruit is really tender.

3 Break down the fruit with a potato masher and leave until cold.

4 Tip the fruit and liquid carefully into a large jelly bag or fine nylon sieve (strainer) suspended over a large mixing bowl and leave to drip for 12–14 hours. You can help it on its way initially by stirring the contents gently round in the bag a few times and even giving the bag an occasional light squeeze to release the juice. Do not exert too much pressure as small fragments of pulp may get through the bag and cloud the jelly.

5 Pour the juices into a measuring jug and make up to 1.2 litres/2 pts/5 cups with cold water. Transfer to a bowl and cook uncovered on Full for 10 minutes.

6 Stir in the sugar and lemon juice and cook on Full for a further 10 minutes until the sugar has dissolved, stirring twice with a wooden spoon.

7 Reduce the power to Medium (550w) and continue to cook for 25–35 minutes until setting point is reached, stirring three or four times.

8 Allow to cool to lukewarm, then ladle into warmed jars, top with paper discs and leave until cold. Cover with lids or cellophane and label the jars.

Quince Jelly with Rose

A clear, honey-coloured jelly that I flavour with rose water for a taste of heaven. You can cook the quinces in a pressure cooker for a speedier result.

makes 1.5 kg/3 lb/3 jars

1 kg/2¼ lb/2 large quinces
2 whole cloves
15 ml/1 tbsp lemon juice
900 ml/1½ pts/3¾ cups boiling water
1.25 kg/2½ lb/5 cups jam sugar
15 ml/1 tbsp rose water

1 Thinly peel the quinces and put the peelings into a piece of muslin (cheesecloth) or other strong cloth. Thinly slice the quinces. Add the cores to the peelings with the cloves. Tie up securely to make a bag.

2 Place the fruit, bag of peelings, lemon juice and boiling water in a 4 litre/7 pt/ 17½ cup capacity bowl, cover and cook on Low or Simmer (450w) for 45 minutes. Allow to rest for 10 minutes, then uncover and continue to cook on Full (750 800w) for 15–25 minutes until tender.

3 Pulp the fruit with a potato masher, then leave until cold.

4 Carefully tip the fruit and liquid into a large jelly bag or fine nylon sieve (strainer) suspended over a large mixing bowl and leave to drip for 12–14 hours.

5 Pour the juices into a measuring jug and make up to 1.2 litres/2 pts/5 cups with cold water if necessary. Return to the original bowl, leave uncovered and cook on Full (750–800w) for 10 minutes.

6 Stir in the sugar and cook on Full for a further 10 minutes, stirring three or four times with a wooden spoon.

7 Reduce the power to Medium (550w) and continue to cook for 30–35 minutes until setting point is reached, stirring three or four times.

8 Mix in the rose water, then allow to cool to lukewarm. Ladle into warmed jars, top with paper discs and leave until cold. Cover with lids or cellophane and label the jars.

Mulled Red Wine Jelly

A jelly that celebrates winter, quite special for the Christmas table, and a marvellous gift for anyone who appreciates home-made luxuries. See photograph opposite page 24.

makes 1.25 kg/2¾ lb/3 jars

1 small orange
1 medium lemon
450 g/1 lb cooking (tart) apples
1 litre/1¾ pts/4¼ cups strong red wine
1 vanilla pod (bean)
1 cinnamon stick
2 whole cloves
700 g/1½ lb/3 cups jam sugar

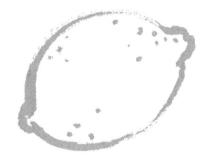

1 Grate (shred) the rind and squeeze the juice of the orange and lemon into a 4 litre/ 7 pt/17½ cup capacity bowl, reserving the pips and pith. Cut up the pith and place in a square of muslin (cheesecloth) or a coffee filter bag with the pips, tie securely and add to the bowl. Cut the apples into smallish pieces without peeling or coring. Add to the bowl with the wine, vanilla pod, cinnamon and cloves.

2 Leave uncovered and cook on Full (750–800w) for 30 minutes.

3 Cover and leave to stand for 2 hours.

4 Strain through a fine mesh sieve (strainer) into a 1.2 litre/2 pt/5 cup measuring jug and squeeze in the juices from the bag of pips and pith. Make up to 900 ml/1½ pts/ 3¾ cups with hot water.

5 Return to the original bowl. Stir in the sugar and and cook on Full for 12 minutes until the sugar has dissolved, stirring three or four times with a wooden spoon.

6 Reduce the power to Medium (550w) and cook for 25–30 minutes until setting point is reached, stirring three or four times.

7 Allow to cool to lukewarm, then ladle into warmed jars, top with paper discs and leave until cold. Cover with lids or cellophane and label the jars.

Redcurrant Jelly

The classic jelly for roast lamb, this home-made version is quite special.

makes 1.5 kg/3 lb/3 jars

1.5 kg/3 lb redcurrants, stalks removed
1.2 litres/2 pts/5 cups boiling water
900 g/2 lb/4 cups jam sugar

1 Put the redcurrants in a 4 litre/7 pt/17½ cup capacity bowl and add the boiling water. Leave uncovered and cook on Full (750–800w) for 12 minutes until the fruit is soft and pulpy, stirring two or three times.

2 Break down the fruit with a potato masher and leave until cold.

3 Carefully tip the fruit and liquid into a large jelly bag or nylon sieve (strainer) suspended over a large mixing bowl and leave to drip for 12–14 hours.

4 Pour the juices into a measuring jug and make up to 1.2 litres/2 pts/5 cups with cold water if necessary.

5 Return to the original bowl, leave uncovered and cook on Full for 10 minutes.

6 Stir in the sugar. Cook on Full for a further 10 minutes until the sugar has dissolved, stirring three or four times with a wooden spoon.

7 Reduce the power to Medium (550w) and continue to cook for 30–35 minutes until setting point is reached, stirring three or four times.

8 Allow to cool to lukewarm, then ladle into warmed jars, top with paper discs and leave until cold. Cover with lids or cellophane and label the jars.

Mixed Currant Jelly

makes 1.5 kg/3 lb/3 jars

Prepare as for Redcurrant Jelly, but use a mixture of redcurrants, blackcurrants and even whitecurrants instead of all red.

Strawberry and Apple Jelly

An exquisite summer jelly to please the heart of every strawberry lover. You can flavour the jelly with 15–30 ml/1–2 tbsp of kirsch or cherry brandy before bottling, or push a few fresh lavender heads into each jar of cold jelly.

makes 1.6 kg/3½ lb/3 large jars

> 700 g/1½ lb cooking (tart) apples
> 450 g/1 lb strawberries, hulled and sliced
> 900 ml/1½ pts/3¾ cups boiling water
> 1 kg/2¼ lb/4½ cups jam sugar

1 Cut the apples into small pieces without peeling or coring. Put into a 4 litre/7 pt/ 17½ cup bowl with the strawberries and 300 ml/½ pt/1¼ cups of the boiling water.

2 Leave uncovered and cook on Full (750–800w) for 10 minutes until soft and pulpy, stirring two or three times.

3 Break down the fruit with a potato masher, stir in the rest of the boiling water and leave until cold.

4 Carefully tip the fruit and liquid into a large jelly bag or nylon sieve (strainer) suspended over a large mixing bowl and leave to drip for 12–14 hours. You can help it on its way initially by stirring the contents gently round in the bag with a spoon a few times and even giving the bag an occasional light squeeze to release the juice. Do not exert too much pressure as small fragments of pulp may get through the bag and cloud the jelly.

5 Pour the juices into a measuring jug and make up to 1.2 litres/2 pts/5 cups with cold water if necessary.

6 Transfer to a bowl and cook uncovered on Full for 10 minutes.

7 Stir in the sugar and cook on Full for 10 minutes, stirring four times.

8 Reduce the power to Medium (550w) and continue to cook for 30–35 minutes until setting point is reached, stirring three or four times.

9 Allow to cool to lukewarm, then ladle into warmed jars, top with paper discs and leave until cold. Cover with lids or cellophane and label the jars.

Conserves

Hovering somewhere between fairly chunky jam and fruits preserved in syrup, conserves are top-notch preserves of memorable taste and may be used as a topping for ice creams, sorbets, yoghurts, milk puddings, bread and butter pudding and simple sweet flans. On the savoury side, they can be served as a condiment with game, poultry and roast pork and mild white cheeses such as goats' cheese.

Coconut Conserve

A speciality from France where it's heavily advertised in the press and very expensive to buy. All the more reason to make your own! It's a bit like old-fashioned coconut ice speckled with brown skin and is popular with lovers of coconut as a topping for vanilla ice cream, a pancake filling and a cake icing (frosting) or even on toast instead of jam or marmalade. See photograph opposite page 96.

makes about 900 g/2 lb/2 jars

2 coconuts
500 g/18 oz/2¼ cups granulated sugar
5 ml/1 tsp vanilla essence (extract)
200 ml/7 fl oz/scant 1 cup apple juice

1 Make a couple of holes in the top of each coconut and pour the clear milk from both coconuts into a measuring jug. Make up to 200 ml/7 fl oz/scant 1 cup with water, then pour into a 3.5 litre/6 pt/15 cup capacity bowl and add the sugar.

2 Prise the flesh out of the coconut shells and break it into small chunks with the brown skin still attached. Finely chop in a food processor.

3 Cook the bowl of milk and sugar, uncovered, on Full (750–800w) for 8 minutes to form a syrup, stirring twice with a wooden spoon.

4 Reduce the power to Medium (550w) and cook for 10 minutes.

5 Add the coconut flesh, vanilla essence and apple juice and continue to cook on Medium for 25–30 minutes until the mixture is thick, stirring four or five times.

6 Allow to cool to lukewarm, then ladle into warmed jars, top with paper discs and leave until cold.

7 Cover with lids or cellophane and label the jars. Store in the refrigerator for up to two months.

> Conserves should be stored in a cool, dark place, or in the fridge if indicated in the recipe, and can be kept up to a year but must be checked regularly at two-month intervals for mildew.

Super-chunky Pink Grapefruit Conserve with Campari

There's nothing nicer than this delightful conserve spooned over steamed and baked puddings, or as a filling in baked apples and pancakes.

makes 1.5 kg/3 lb/3 jars

2 pink- or red-fleshed grapefruit
1 medium lemon
1.2 litres/2 pts/5 cups boiling water
1.25 kg /2½ lb/5 cups granulated sugar
30 ml/2 tbsp Campari

1 Put the grapefruit and lemon on a glass plate and cook on Full (750–800w) for 3–4 minutes. Halve the fruits, put in a 4 litre/7 pt/17½ cup capacity bowl and add the boiling water. Part-cover the bowl with a perforated plastic lid or plate and cook on Medium (550w) for 35 minutes until soft.

2 Remove the fruit from the bowl with a draining spoon, letting any liquid run back into the bowl. Return the fruit halves to the plate and cut into strips with the pith. Don't make the strips too narrow. Discard the pips and any coarse membranes.

3 Return to the bowl of liquid, cover and cook on Medium for 20 minutes to soften the pith still further.

4 Stir in the sugar and continue to cook on Medium for 35 minutes until setting point is reached, stirring frequently at the beginning to make sure the sugar dissolves, then stirring a further three or four times with a wooden spoon during cooking.

5 Stir in the Campari.

6 Allow to cool to lukewarm, then ladle into warmed jars, top with paper discs and leave until cold.

7 Cover with lids or cellophane and label the jars.

Papaya and Lime Conserve with Southern Comfort

An incredible-tasting conserve, deeply fragrant and beautifully pink.

makes 1.5 kg/3 lb/3 jars

4 large just-ripe papayas, about 1.6 kg/3½ lb prepared weight
Finely grated (shredded) peel and juice of 2 washed and dried limes
45 ml/3 tbsp water
750 g/1¾ lb/3½ cups jam sugar
30 ml/2 tbsp Southern Comfort

1 Peel the papaya and remove the seeds. Cut the flesh into small dice and put in a 4.5 litre/8 pt/20 cup capacity bowl. Add all the remaining ingredients except the Southern Comfort and leave to stand for 30 minutes.

2 Cook uncovered on Full (750–800w) for 15 minutes until the sugar has dissolved, stirring three times with a wooden spoon.

3 Reduce the power to Medium (550w) and continue to cook for a further 25–30 minutes until setting point is reached, stirring three or four times.

4 Stir in the Southern Comfort.

5 Allow to cool to lukewarm, then ladle into warmed jars, top with paper discs and leave until cold.

6 Cover with lids or cellophane and label the jars.

Opposite: Coconut Conserve (page 94)
Overleaf: Lemon and Lime Curd (pages 108–9)

Pear Conserve with Saffron

This combination of three types of pear with perry (pear cider) and yellow saffron is exquisite and, as far as I know, unique. The total weight of the pears should be about 1 kg/2¼ lb.

makes 1.5 kg/3 lb/3 jars

5 ml/1 tsp saffron strands

60 ml/4 tbsp boiling water

2 William pears, peeled, cored and coarsely chopped

1 conference pear, peeled, cored and coarsely chopped

2 Japanese nashi pears, peeled, cored and coarsely chopped

250 ml/8 fl oz/1 cup sparkling perry

15 ml/1 tbsp lemon juice

1 kg/2¼ lb/4½ cups jam sugar

1 Soak the saffron in the boiling water in a small bowl for 30 minutes.

2 Put the pears, perry, lemon juice, saffron and soaking water in a 4 litre/ 7 pt/17½ cup bowl. Leave uncovered and cook on Full (750–800w) for 10 minutes.

3 Stir in the sugar and cook on Full for 10 minutes, stirring three or four times with a wooden spoon.

4 Reduce the power to Medium (550w) and continue to cook for a further 25–30 minutes until setting point is reached, stirring three or four times.

5 Allow to cool to lukewarm, then ladle into warmed jars, top with paper discs and leave until cold.

6 Cover with lids or cellophane and label the jars.

Opposite: *Fresh Figs with Orange Strips in Bourbon (page 116)*
Overleaf: *Sweet and Sour Red Cabbage Pickle (page 146) and Carrot and Coriander Relish (page 141)*

Rhubarb and Ginger Wine Conserve

For those who like the tang of ginger, this is a wonderful conserve to go with both sweet and savoury dishes. As a matter of culinary interest, Balkan countries serve little dishes of home-made conserve with glasses of cold water at teatime. In Yugoslavia, for instance, the conserve is called *slatko*. In Russia, conserves are often stirred into tea instead of sugar for added sweetness, colour and flavour.

makes 900 g/2 lb/2 jars

> 700 g/1½ lb rhubarb, trimmed and cut into 1 cm/½ in pieces
> 90 ml/6 tbsp lemon juice
> 700 g/1½ lb/3 cups jam sugar
> 15 ml/1 tbsp ginger wine

1 Put all the ingredients except the ginger wine in a 4.5 litre/8 pt/20 cup capacity bowl and leave to stand for 24 hours.

2 Cook uncovered on Full (750–800w) for 15 minutes until the sugar has dissolved, stirring three times with a wooden spoon.

3 Reduce the power to Medium (550w) and continue to cook for a further 35–40 minutes until setting point is reached, stirring three or four times.

4 Stir in the ginger wine.

5 Allow to cool to lukewarm, then ladle into warmed jars, top with paper discs and leave until cold.

6 Cover with lids or cellophane and label the jars.

Mincemeats

Mincemeats and mince pies date back as far as the

sixteenth century when they were known as mutton

pies after the minced mutton or lamb generally

contained in the fruit mixture. Now they are quite different

and have evolved into rather more adventurous

mixes of fruit with butter, margarine and suet – distinctions

with a difference that make for more palatable and

appetising results to suit modern tastes.

All-fruit Mincemeat

Make this glorious, fat-free mincemeat in the summer when the fruits are in season and treasure it for the winter months.

makes 1.6 kg/3½ lb/3 large jars

900 g/2 lb firm nectarines, halved and stoned (pitted)
1 medium eating (dessert) apple, 100 g/4 oz, unpeeled, quartered and cored
175 g/6 oz/1 cup raisins
175 g/6 oz/1 cup dates, chopped
200 g/7 oz/generous 1 cup chopped mixed (candied) peel
Finely grated (shredded) peel and juice of 1 medium orange
Finely grated (shredded) peel and juice of 1 medium lemon
300 ml/½ pt/1¼ cups orange juice
10 ml/2 tsp allspice
225 g/8 oz/1 cup soft light brown or demerara sugar

1 Chop the nectarines and apples fairly finely, either by hand or in a food processor, then put in a 3.5 litre/6 pt/15 cup capacity bowl and add all the remaining ingredients.

2 Leave uncovered and cook on Full (750–800w) for 35 minutes, stirring three or four times with a wooden spoon.

3 Allow to cool to lukewarm, then ladle into warmed jars, top with paper discs and leave until cold.

4 Cover with lids or cellophane and label the jars.

5 Keep in a cool, dark place for up to one month, or up to three months in the fridge.

Vegetarian Mincemeat with Apples

A fat-free mincemeat that is well fruited and laced with alcohol and also very easy to make.

makes 1 kg/2¼ lb/2 jars

450 g/1 lb cooking (tart) apples, peeled, cored and thinly sliced
15 ml/1 tbsp apple juice
225 g/8 oz/1 cup soft dark brown sugar
15 ml/1 tbsp black treacle (molasses)
10 ml/2 tsp mixed (apple-pie) spice
5 ml/1 tsp finely grated (shredded) orange peel
225 g/8 oz/1⅓ cups raisins
225 g/8 oz/1⅓ cups sultanas (golden raisins)
225 g/8 oz/1⅓ cups currants
30 ml/2 tbsp rum or brandy

1 Put the apples and apple juice in a 2.25 litre/4 pt/10 cup capacity bowl. Cover and cook on Full (750–800w) for 8–10 minutes until soft and pulpy, stirring three times with a wooden spoon.

2 Break down in the bowl with a potato masher, then mix in all the remaining ingredients.

3 Allow to cool to lukewarm, then ladle into warmed jars, top with paper discs and leave until cold.

4 Cover with lids or cellophane and label the jars.

5 Store in a cool, dark place for up to 3 months, or almost indefinitely in the fridge.

Buttered Mincemeat with Banana

A Christmas blessing, a dark and succulent mincemeat with a unique trace of butterscotch. The selection of fruit is up to you: try a combination of sultanas (golden raisins), currants, chopped dates and/or stoned (pitted) prunes, raisins, chopped mixed (candied) peel and fruits such as glacé (candied) pineapple.

makes 1.25 kg/2½ lb/2 large jars

100 g/4 oz/½ cup butter

100g/4 oz/½ cup soft dark brown sugar

Finely grated (shredded) peel of 1 pink grapefruit

1 medium eating (dessert) apple, 100 g/4 oz, peeled and grated (shredded)

100 g/4 oz/⅔ cup sugar-rolled dates

1 large, ripe banana, about 225 g/8 oz, peeled and mashed

450 g/1 lb/2⅔ cups mixed dried fruits, including peel

10 ml/2 tsp mixed (apple-pie) spice

30 ml/2 tbsp whisky or brandy

1 Put the butter, sugar and grapefruit peel in a 3 litre/5 pt/12½ cup capacity bowl. Leave uncovered and cook on Defrost, Simmer or Medium-low (270–300w) for about 3–4 minutes until the butter has melted.

2 Stir in all the remaining ingredients.

3 Ladle into warmed jars, top with paper discs and leave until cold.

4 Cover with lids or cellophane and label the jars.

5 Store in the fridge up to four weeks.

Cranberry and Citrus Mincemeat

Dusky rose-coloured with black speckles and gently spiced, this is an entirely new concept in mincemeat combinations and works superbly. As with the Fat-free Fresh Grape Mincemeat (see page 104), you can use any mixture of dried fruit, such as sultanas (golden raisins), currants, chopped dates and/or prunes, raisins, chopped mixed (candied) peel and fruits such as glacé (candied) pineapple. You can also make the mincemeat with blueberries instead of cranberries.

makes 900 g/2 lb/2 jars

100 g/4 oz fresh or frozen and defrosted cranberries
225 g/8 oz cooking (tart) apples, peeled, cored and grated (shredded)
175 g/6 oz/1 cup stoned (pitted) prunes, chopped
175 g/6 oz/³⁄₄ cup soft light brown sugar
175 g/6 oz/1 cup mixed dried fruit
175 g/6 oz/³⁄₄ cup shredded (chopped) beef or vegetarian suet
10 ml/2 tsp mixed (apple-pie) spice
Finely grated (shredded) peel of 1 medium orange

1 Put the cranberries, grated apples and prunes in a 2.25 litre/4 pt/10 cup capacity bowl and mix well. Add all the remaining ingredients.

2 Leave uncovered and cook on Full (750–800w) for 5 minutes, stirring twice with a wooden spoon.

3 Allow to cool to lukewarm, then ladle into warmed jars, top with paper discs and leave until cold.

4 Cover with lids or cellophane and label the jars.

5 Keep in a cool, dark place for up to three months, or up to six months in the fridge.

Fat-free Fresh Grape Mincemeat

A warm and spicy mincemeat spiked with allspice and with grapes taking the place of the usual fat. This is another recipe to please vegetarians and those who want something more slimming than standard mincemeat. You can use any mixture of dried fruit, such as sultanas (golden raisins), currants, chopped dates and/or stoned (pitted) prunes, raisins, chopped mixed (candied) peel and fruits such as glacé (candied) pineapple. See photograph opposite page 73.

makes 1.25 kg/2½ lb/2 large jars

700 g/1½ lb mixed dried fruits, including peel
225 g/8 oz/1 cup soft light brown sugar
2–3 sweet eating (dessert) apples, such as Cox's, about 350 g/12 oz, peeled, cored
   and grated (shredded)
225 g/8 oz green seedless grapes, halved
10 ml/2 tsp allspice
Finely grated (shredded) peel of 1 medium lemon

1 Put the dried fruit, sugar, grated apples, grapes and allspice in a 3 litre/5 pt/12½ cup capacity bowl and mix well.

2 Leave uncovered and cook on Full (750–800w) for 5 minutes, stirring three times with a wooden spoon.

3 Stir in the lemon peel.

4 Allow to cool to lukewarm, then ladle into warmed jars, top with paper discs and leave until cold.

5 Cover with lids or cellophane and label the jars.

6 Keep in a cool, dark place for up to three months, or almost indefinitely in the fridge.

Marmalade Mincemeat

Another buttery mincemeat, the flavour of this preserve is heightened with dark marmalade and dark rum. Use a combination of fruits as you like, selecting from raisins, sultanas (golden raisins), currants, chopped dates, stoned (pitted) prunes and glacé (candied) fruits.

makes 700 g/1½ lb/2 small jars

100 g/4 oz/½ cup butter or margarine
500 g/1 lb 2 oz/3 cups mixed dried fruits without peel
50 g/2 oz/⅙ cup dark orange marmalade
225 g/8 oz/1 cup soft dark brown sugar
5 ml/1 tsp allspice
5 ml/1 tsp finely grated (shredded) orange peel
60 ml/4 tbsp dark rum

1 Put the butter or margarine in a 2.25 litre/4 pt/10 cup capacity bowl and melt, uncovered, on Defrost, Simmer or Medium-low (270–300w) for 3–4 minutes, uncovered.

2 Thoroughly stir in all the remaining ingredients.

3 Allow to cool to lukewarm, then ladle into warmed jars, top with paper discs and leave until cold.

4 Cover with lids or cellophane and label the jars.

5 Store in the fridge for up to six weeks.

Curds and Butters

Essentially, all the recipes in this chapter make **beautiful** spreads. They are mostly quite thick, some opaque, others dense but rarely **translucent** in the same way as a fruit jelly like redcurrant or apple. A good example is Classic Lemon Curd, made simply from fruit pulp and sugar. The fruit butters themselves make **sophisticated** and expensive-tasting **condiments** and can be served with grilled (broiled) meals and roasts of meat, poultry, game and liver and also with grilled oily fish such as mackerel, herring and tuna, which benefit from a fruity side-kick.

Classic Lemon Curd

The eternal lemony classic based on butter, lemon and eggs. This takes just a few minutes to make in the microwave and turns out thick, golden and velvety smooth. For a less tangy taste, increase the quantity of sugar by 50 g/2 oz/¼ cup. See photograph overleaf from page 96.

makes 750 g/1¾ lb/2 small jars

300 g/10 oz/1¼ cups caster (superfine) sugar
Finely grated (shredded) peel of 4 lemons
150 ml/¼ pt/⅔ cup lemon juice
100 g/4 oz/½ cup butter, diced and slightly softened
4 large eggs, at room temperature

1 Put the sugar, lemon peel and juice in a 1.75 litre/3 pt/7½ cup bowl. Cook on Full (750–800w) for 5 minutes.

2 Remove the bowl from the microwave, add the butter and stir until melted. Allow an extra 30 seconds cooking time to melt the butter if necessary.

3 In a separate bowl, thoroughly whisk the eggs, then gradually beat the eggs into the lemon mixture.

4 Cook, uncovered, on Medium (550w) for 5–6 minutes, beating hard with a wooden spoon at the end of every minute. When ready, the curd should be really thick and glossy. If not, allow a few seconds more cooking time.

5 Spoon into warmed jars, top with paper discs and leave until cold.

6 Cover with lids or cellophane and label the jars.

7 Store in the fridge for up to six weeks.

Lemon Curd with Mint

makes 750 g/1¾ lb/2 small jars

Prepare as for Classic Lemon Curd, but stir in 15 ml/1 tbsp very finely chopped fresh or frozen mint before bottling.

Lemon Curd with Nutmeg

makes 750 g/1¾ lb/2 small jars

Prepare as for Classic Lemon Curd, but stir in 5 ml/1 tsp freshly grated nutmeg before bottling.

Orange and Lemon Curd

makes 750 g/1¾ lb/2 small jars

Prepare as for Classic Lemon Curd, but use the grated (shredded) peel and juice of 1 orange and 2 lemons instead of all lemon peel.

Lime Curd

makes 750 g/1¾ lb/2 small jars

Prepare as for Classic Lemon Curd, but use 5 limes instead of 4 lemons. See photograph overleaf from page 96.

Coconut Honey Curd

Preserves based on coconut are very popular in Europe, and this outstanding coconut recipe tastes and looks like honey made from coconut flowers. Use it instead of honey as a spread, in dressings and bastes, and in sweet-and-sour sauces, but not generally in baking.

makes about 1.25 kg/2½ lb/2 large jars

2 x 400 ml/2 x 14 fl oz/2 large cans of coconut milk
60 ml/4 tbsp lemon juice
200 ml/7 fl oz/1 carton UHT coconut cream
750 g/1¾ lb/3½ cups jam sugar

1 Put all the ingredients in a 2.25 litre/4 pt/10 cup capacity bowl. Leave uncovered and cook on Full (750–800w) for 18 minutes until the sugar has dissolved, stirring four times with a wooden spoon.

2 Reduce the power to Medium (550w) and continue to cook for a further 25–30 minutes, stirring four times, until the mixture is thick and curd-like.

3 Allow to cool to lukewarm, then ladle into warmed jars, top with paper discs and leave until cold.

4 Cover with lids or cellophane and label the jars.

5 Store in a cool, dark place for up to three months. The curd might separate out into two layers on standing so stir round before use.

Apple Butter

A lingering, fruity taste typifies this smooth, thick and slightly spicy opaque spread which is firm and not over-sweet.

makes 750 g/1¾ lb/2 small jars

900 g/2 lb cooking (tart) apples, peeled, cored and sliced
15 ml/1 tbsp lemon juice
150 ml/¼ pt/⅔ cup apple juice
400 g/14 oz/1¾ cups granulated sugar
5 ml/1 tsp mixed (apple-pie) spice

1 Put the apples, lemon juice and apple juice in a 3 litre/5 pt/12½ cup capacity bowl. Cover and cook on Full (750–800w) for 10 minutes, stirring three times with a wooden spoon.

2 Purée until smooth in a blender or food processor.

3 Return the purée (paste) to the original bowl and stir in the sugar and spice. Cook on Full for a further 7 minutes until the sugar has dissolved, stirring three times.

4 Reduce the power Medium (550w) and continue to cook for about 18–20 minutes until the preserve is very thick, stirring frequently and carefully as the preserve tends to splutter.

5 Allow to cool to lukewarm, then ladle into warmed jars, top with paper discs and leave until cold.

6 Cover with lids or cellophane and label the jars. Store in a cool, dark place for up to a year.

Pear Butter

makes 750 g/1¾ lb/2 small jars

Prepare as for Apple Butter, but use the same weight of prepared pears instead of apples.

Plum Butter

makes 750 g/1¾ lb/2 small jars

Prepare as for Apple Butter (see page 111), but use the same weight of stoned (pitted) ripe dark plums instead of apples.

Persimmon Butter

A seductive and exotic recipe. See photograph opposite page 24.

makes 750 g/1¾ lb/2 small jars

750 g/1¾ lb persimmons
Grated peel and juice of 1 lime
30 ml/2 tbsp lemon juice
450 g/1 lb/2 cups granulated sugar

1 Remove the small calyx at the top of each persimmon and discard any bruised flesh. Cut up, with skins, and purée in a food processor.

2 Put all the ingredients in a 3 litre/5 pt/12½ cup capacity bowl. Cover and cook on Full (750–800w) for 10 minutes until the sugar has dissolved, stirring three times with a wooden spoon.

3 Reduce the power Medium (550w) and continue to cook for about 30–40 minutes until the preserve is very thick, stirring frequently and carefully as the preserve tends to splutter.

4 Allow to cool to lukewarm, then ladle into warmed jars, top with paper discs and leave until cold.

5 Cover with lids or cellophane and label the jars.

6 Store in a cool, dark place for up to a year.

Fruits in Alcohol

Fruits in alcohol have always been the élite of the preserve family, but if you are bowled over by shop prices, make your own by this reliable microwave method.

Dried Apricots in Amaretto

Amaretto di Soronno is a traditional Italian almond liqueur that is readily available in supermarkets and off-licences (liquor stores).

makes one 1.2 litre/2 pt/5 cup jar

500 g/18 oz/3 cups dried apricots
Hot water
300 ml/$^1/_2$ pt/1$^1/_4$ cups orange juice
150 g/5 oz/$^2/_3$ cup caster (superfine) sugar
4 whole allspice
About 250 ml/8 fl oz/1 cup amaretto liqueur

1 Cover the apricots in hot water and leave to soak for 2 hours, then drain well.

2 Put the apricots, orange juice and sugar in a 1.75 litre/3 pt/7$^1/_2$ cup capacity bowl. Leave uncovered and cook on Medium (550w) for 7 minutes, stirring once with a wooden spoon.

3 Transfer to a 1.2 litre/2 pt/5 cup capacity jar, add the allspice and top up with amaretto.

4 Cover securely with a double thickness of microwave wrap (plastic wrap) and a well-fitting lid and label the jar.

5 Store in a cool, dark place for up to a year.

Fresh Figs in Sweet White Wine with Mace

Eat these for dessert with plain sponge fingers, crème fraîche or something like an almond tart or cheesecake.

makes one 900 ml/1½ pt/3¾ cup jar

7–8 fresh, fleshy figs, not too big
375 ml/13 fl oz/1⅔ cups sweet white dessert wine
2 blades of mace, broken into pieces

1 Put the figs in a 900 ml/1½ pt/3¾ cup capacity jar with a fairly wide neck and three-quarters fill with wine. Add the mace.

2 Heat the jar and contents on Full (750–800w) for 4 minutes.

3 Fill to the brim with the rest of the wine, then leave to cool.

4 Cover securely with a double thickness of microwave wrap (plastic wrap) and a well-fitting lid and label the jar.

5 Store in a cook, dark place for up to a year.

Fresh Figs with Orange Strips in Bourbon

The bouquet from this preserve is positively haunting and mystical and, once the figs have been eaten, the syrup can be diluted with well-chilled sparkling white wine or mineral water to make a long, cold drink. See photograph opposite page 97.

makes one 1.2 litre/2 pt/5 cup jar

1 tangerine-type fruit
8 large fresh figs
100 g/4 oz/$\frac{1}{2}$ cup caster (superfine) sugar
2 star anise
2 cinnamon sticks
250 ml/8 fl oz/1 cup Bourbon

1 Thinly pare the peel from the tangerine and cut into thin strips. Reserve.

2 Put the figs in a 1.5 litre/2$\frac{1}{2}$ pt/6 cup capacity bowl and gently toss with the sugar until every piece of fruit is well coated.

3 Cook on Full (750–800w) for 3$\frac{1}{2}$ minutes.

4 Leave to stand for 20 minutes.

5 Transfer the fruit to a 1.2 litre/2 pt/5 cup capacity jar and add all the remaining ingredients and the tangerine peel.

6 Cover securely with a double thickness of microwave wrap (plastic wrap) and a well-fitting lid. Label the jar.

7 Store in a cool, dark place for up to a year.

Dried Figs with Vanilla in Calvados

If possible, use pale yellow Greek or Turkish figs for this recipe.

makes one 1.2 litre/2 pt/5 cup jar

500 g/18 oz/3 cups dried figs
300 ml/$\frac{1}{2}$ pt/1$\frac{1}{4}$ cups apple juice
150 g/5 oz/$\frac{2}{3}$ cup caster (superfine) sugar
2 vanilla pods (beans)
About 250 ml/8 fl oz/1 cup calvados

1 Put the figs, apple juice and sugar in a 1.75 litre/3 pt/7$\frac{1}{2}$ cup capacity bowl. Leave uncovered and cook on Medium (550w) for 7 minutes, stirring once with a wooden spoon.

2 Transfer to a 1.2 litre/2 pt/5 cup capacity jar, add the vanilla pods and top up with calvados.

3 Cover securely with a double thickness of microwave wrap (plastic wrap) and a well-fitting lid and label the jar.

4 Store in a cool, dark place for up to a year.

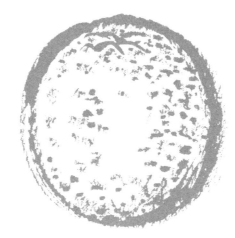

Physalis with Lemon in White Rum

A one-off – an elegant preserve with unexpected highlights.

makes two 350 ml/12 fl oz/1½ cup jars

400 g/14 oz physalis, husks removed
100 g/4 oz/½ cup caster (superfine) sugar
Strips of peel from 1 medium lemon
120–150 ml/4–5 fl oz/½–⅔ cup white rum

1 Put the physalis and sugar in a 1.5 litre/2½ pt/6 cup capacity bowl and toss until well mixed.

2 Cook on Medium (550w) for 3½ minutes.

3 Divide equally between two 350 ml/12 fluid oz/1½ cup capacity jars, adding half the lemon peel to each. Top up the jars to the brim with rum.

4 Cover each jar securely with a double thickness of microwave wrap (plastic wrap) and a well-fitting lid and label the jars.

5 Store in a cool, dark place for up to a year.

Prunes with Allspice in Brandy

A French speciality and a beloved dessert from south-west France. Eat the prunes, then sip the syrup from a liqueur glass.

makes one 1.2 litre/2 pt/5 cup jar

500 g/18 oz/3 cups stoned (pitted) prunes
300 ml/^{1}/$_2$ pt/1^1/$_4$ cups grape juice
150 g/5 oz/^{2}/$_3$ cup caster (superfine) sugar
4 whole allspice
About 250 ml/8 fl oz/1 cup brandy

1 Put the prunes, grape juice and sugar in a 1.75 litre/3 pt/7^1/$_2$ cup capacity bowl. Leave uncovered and cook on Medium (550w) for 7 minutes, stirring once with a wooden spoon.

2 Transfer to a 1.2 litre/2 pt/5 cup capacity jar, add the allspice and top up with brandy.

3 Cover securely with a double thickness of microwave wrap (plastic wrap) and a well-fitting lid and label the jar.

4 Store In a cool, dark place for up to a year.

Star Fruit and Blueberries in Gin

The star of the show, serve this divine drink in liqueur glasses with the two fruits at the end of a meal, or top up the flavoured gin with chilled lemonade for a scintillating spritzer. See photograph opposite.

makes two 200 ml/7 fl oz/scant 1 cup jars

2 star fruit, very thinly sliced and seeded
100 g/4 oz blueberries
100 g/4 oz/$\frac{1}{2}$ cup caster (superfine) sugar
Strips of peel from 1 medium lemon
120–150 ml/4–5 fl oz/$\frac{1}{2}$–$\frac{2}{3}$ cup gin

1 Put the star fruit, blueberries and sugar in a 1.5 litre/2$\frac{1}{2}$ pt/6 cup capacity bowl and toss until well mixed.

2 Cook on Medium (550w) for 2$\frac{1}{2}$ minutes.

3 Divide equally between two 200 ml/7 fl oz/scant 1 cup capacity jars, adding half the lemon peel to each. Top up the jars to the brim with gin.

4 Cover each jar securely with a double thickness of microwave wrap (plastic wrap) and a well-fitting lid and label the jars.

5 Store in a cool, dark place for up to a year.

Opposite: *Star Fruit and Blueberries in Gin*

Chutneys

Chutney, the essential sweet-sour pickle in British households and in every pub that serves a ploughman's lunch, has been with us since the days of the Raj, when it was known to the British as *chutnee* and custom has allowed us to introduce the term, as well as all that embraces, into the English language.

Opposite: *Mango and Papaya Chutney (page 129)*

Apple Chutney

Chutney responds well to microwave treatment and this is a great-tasting one. Add the cayenne pepper if you like a chutney with a bit of heat.

makes 900 g/2 lb/2 jars

450 g/1 lb cooking (tart) apples, peeled, cored and chopped

1 large onion, grated (shredded)

15 ml/1 tbsp salt

450 ml/³⁄₄ pt/2 cups malt or cider vinegar

225 g/8 oz/1 cup dark brown soft sugar

2–3 garlic cloves, sliced

100 g/4 oz/²⁄₃ cup dates, chopped

100 g/4 oz/²⁄₃ cup raisins, chopped

15 ml/1 tbsp ground ginger

5 ml/1 tsp ground cinnamon

5 ml/1 tsp mixed (apple-pie) spice

1.5–5 ml/¹⁄₄–1 tsp cayenne pepper (optional)

15 ml/1 tbsp mixed pickling spice

1 bay leaf

2 star anise

2.5 cm/1 in piece of cinnamon stick

1 Put the apples and onion in a 4 litre/7 pt/17¹⁄₂ cup capacity bowl with the salt and vinegar. Leave uncovered and and cook on Full (750–800w) for 5 minutes, stirring once with a wooden spoon.

2 Stir in the sugar, garlic, dates, raisins, ginger, cinnamon and mixed spice.

3 Tie the remaining ingredients in a piece of muslin (cheesecloth) or twist securely in a large coffee filter paper bag. Add to the bowl.

4 Leave uncovered and cook on Full for 30–40 minutes until the chutney thickens to a jam-like consistency, stirring three or four times with a wooden spoon. If the chutney is too runny, cook for an extra 5–10 minutes until it reaches the desired thickness.

5 Remove and discard the bag of spices.

6 Allow to cool to lukewarm, then ladle into warmed jars, top with paper discs and leave until cold.

7 Cover with non-metallic lids or cellophane and label the jars.

Apple and Pear Chutney

makes 900 g/2 lb/2 jars

Prepare as for Apple Chutney, but use half apples and half pears.

Apple, Red Tomato and Apricot Chutney

makes 900 g/2 lb/2 jars

Prepare as for Apple Chutney, but use half apples and half red tomatoes. Substitute chopped dried apricots for the raisins.

Dark Plum Chutney

makes 900 g/2 lb/2 jars

Prepare as for Apple Chutney, but substitute stoned (pitted) dark plums (prepared weight) for the apples.

Chutneys should be stored in a cool, dark place and can be kept for up to a year but should be checked regularly for mildew at two-month intervals.

Apple and Celery Chutney

A simple but delicious chutney, smartly spiced.

makes 1.5 kg/3 lb/3 jars

1.25 kg/2½ lb cooking (tart) apples, peeled, cored and chopped (900 g/2 lb prepared
weight)

150 g/6 oz/3 celery sticks

2 large onions, each cut into eighths

3 garlic cloves

175 g/6 oz/1 cup raisins

450 ml/¾ pt/2 cups malt or cider vinegar

350 g/12 oz/1½ cups soft light brown sugar

10 ml/2 tsp salt

1.5–5 ml/¼–1 tsp chilli powder

2.5 ml/½ tsp mixed (apple-pie) spice

2.5 ml/½ tsp ground ginger

5 ml/1 tsp celery salt

1 Coarsely chop the apples, celery, onions, garlic and raisins in a food processor, then scrape into a 4 litre/7 pt/17½ cup capacity bowl and stir in the vinegar.

2 Leave uncovered and cook on Full (750–800w) for 20 minutes, stirring three times with a wooden spoon.

3 Add all the remaining ingredients and mix in well. Leave uncovered and continue to cook on Full for 25–35 minutes until the chutney thickens to a jam-like consistency, stirring four or five times. If the chutney is too runny, cook for an extra 5–10 minutes until it reaches the desired thickness.

4 Allow to cool to lukewarm, then ladle into warmed jars, top with paper discs and leave until cold.

5 Cover with non-metallic lids or cellophane and label the jars.

Apple and Red Tomato Chutney with Dried Peaches

A warm-hearted and friendly chutney, bursting with sunshine flavours and hotted up with just enough bird's eye chillies for you to know they're there.

makes 1.5 kg/3 lb/3 jars

175 g/6 oz/1 cup no-need-to-soak dried peaches

550 g/1¼ lb cooking (tart) apples, peeled, cored and chopped (450 g/1 lb prepared weight)

2 medium onions, thickly sliced

450 g/1 lb tomatoes, skinned

3 garlic cloves

450 ml/¾ pt/2 cups light malt vinegar

3 dried or fresh bird's eye chillies

2.5 ml/½ tsp ground cinnamon

2.5 ml/½ tsp freshly grated nutmeg

15 ml/1 tbsp sun-dried tomato paste

10–15 ml/2–3 tsp salt

350 g/12 oz/1½ cups soft light brown sugar

1 Coarsely chop the peaches, apples, onions, tomatoes and garlic in a food processor, then scrape into a 4 litre/7 pt/17½ cup capacity bowl and add all the remaining ingredients except the sugar. Mix in well.

2 Leave uncovered and cook on Full (750–800w) for 25 minutes, stirring three times with a wooden spoon.

3 Add the sugar and continue to cook on Full for a further 20–25 minutes until the chutney thickens to a jam-like consistency, stirring three or four times. If the chutney is too runny, cook for an extra 5–10 minutes until it reaches the desired thickness.

4 Allow to cool to lukewarm, then ladle into warmed jars, top with paper discs and leave until cold.

5 Cover with non-metallic lids or cellophane and label the jars.

Anglo-Indian Apple Chutney

An outstandingly piquant condiment with background flavours reminiscent of the best in Indian preserves. This chutney is very dark and sweeter than most. Chutney proper, as manufactured in India, is a powerful condiment prepared by mixing a variety of fruits, sugar, vinegar and spices so cleverly that all the flavours work together with no one flavour predominating.

makes 1.6 kg/3½ lb/3 large jars

6 garlic cloves, sliced

50 g/2 oz fresh root ginger, sliced

900 g/2 lb cooking (tart) apples, peeled, cored and cut into chunks

25 g/1 oz fresh coriander (cilantro)

3 fresh bird's eye chillies

600 ml/1 pt/2½ cups malt vinegar

15 ml/1 tbsp salt

10 ml/2 tsp yellow mustard seeds

225 g/8 oz sugar-rolled dates

10 ml/2 tsp garam masala

700 g/1½ lb/3 cups golden granulated sugar

1 Coarsely chop the garlic, ginger, apples and coriander in a food processor, then transfer to a 4 litre/7 pt/17½ cup capacity bowl and add the chillies, half the vinegar and all remaining ingredients except the sugar.

2 Leave uncovered and cook on Full (750–800w) for 20 minutes, stirring two or three times with a wooden spoon.

3 Stir in the remaining vinegar and the sugar.

4 Continue to cook on Full for about 30 minutes until the chutney thickens to a jam-like consistency, stirring about four times.

5 Allow to cool to lukewarm, then ladle into warmed jars, top with paper discs and leave until cold.

6 Cover with non-metallic lids or cellophane and label the jars.

Banana Chutney with Tomatoes and Peppers

A chutney for discerning palates, this has an appetising texture and is good served with cold meats and crusty bread.

makes 1.5 kg/3 lb/3 jars

2 large onions, cut into eighths

1 small orange (bell) pepper, seeded

1 small yellow (bell) pepper, seeded

2–3 garlic cloves, halved

4 medium tomatoes, skinned

1.5 kg/3 lb ripe yellow bananas

100 g/4 oz/²⁄₃ cup raisins

Juice of ¹⁄₂ lemon

175 ml/6 fl oz/³⁄₄ cup malt vinegar

100 g/4 oz/¹⁄₂ cup soft dark brown sugar

2–3 tsp salt

2 whole cloves

1 bay leaf

5 ml/1 tsp ground ginger

15 ml/1 tbsp Worcestershire sauce

1 Coarsely chop the onions, peppers and garlic in a food processor. Pulse in the tomatoes and peeled bananas. Transfer to a 4 litre/7 pt/17¹⁄₂ cup capacity bowl and add all the remaining ingredients.

2 Leave uncovered and cook on Full (750–800w) for 10 minutes, stirring twice with a wooden spoon.

3 Reduce the power to Medium (550w) and continue to cook for 40–45 minutes until the chutney thickens to a jam-like consistency, stirring four or five times.

4 Cool to lukewarm, then remove the bay leaf. Ladle into warmed jars, top with paper discs and leave until cold.

5 Cover with non-metallic lids or cellophane and label the jars.

Beetroot and Apple Chutney

I have a friend, Adrian, who is head chef at one of the Wagamama chain of Japanese-style fast-food restaurants in Central London. When he's not tangled up with noodles and seaweed, he turns out some thought-provoking chutneys, like this one based on red onions and beetroot with a trace of apple.

makes 1.5 kg/3 lb/3 jars

225 g/8 oz red onions, chopped

300 ml/½ pt/1¼ cups malt vinegar

1 bay leaf

5 ml/1 tsp white mustard seed

2.5 ml/½ tsp coarsely ground black pepper

2 medium eating (dessert) apples, such as Cox's, peeled, cored and quartered

700 g/1½ lb cooked beetroot (red beets), skinned

10–15 ml/2–3 tsp salt

100 g/4 oz/⅔ cup raisins

225 g/8 oz/1 cup soft light brown sugar

1 Put the onions and half the vinegar in a 4 litre/7 pt/17½ cup capacity bowl. Cook on Full (750–800w) for 5 minutes.

2 Mix in the bay leaf, mustard seeds and pepper and leave to stand while you prepare the fruit.

3 Coarsely chop the apples in food processor, then pulse in the beetroot. Scrape into the bowl of onions with all the remaining ingredients, including the remaining vinegar. Leave uncovered and cook on Full for 35–40 minutes until the chutney thickens to a jam-like consistency, stirring four or five times with a wooden spoon. If the chutney is too runny, cook for an extra 5–10 minutes until it reaches the desired thickness.

4 Allow to cool to lukewarm, then ladle into warmed jars, top with paper discs and leave to cool.

5 Cover with non-metallic lids or cellophane and label the jars.

Mango and Papaya Chutney

An exciting use of exotic fruits and a wonderful chutney for Indian, Malaysian and Thai food. See photograph opposite page 121.

makes 1 kg/2¼ lb/2 large jars

300 ml/½ pt/1¼ cups spiced malt vinegar
350 g/12 oz/1½ cups soft light brown sugar
2 large slightly under-ripe mangoes
4 medium papayas
3 fresh tamarind, brittle skins and inside strings removed
2.5 ml/½ tsp freshly grated nutmeg
7.5 ml/1½ tsp salt
50 g/2 oz/⅓ cup raisins or sultanas (golden raisins)
Finely grated peel of 1 large lemon
10 ml/2 tsp liquid acetic acid

1 Put the vinegar and sugar in a 3 litre/5 pt/12½ cup capacity bowl.

2 Peel the mangoes and cut the flesh away from stones (pits). Coarsely chop the flesh and add to the bowl. Leave uncovered and cook on Medium (550w) for 20–25 minutes until the mixture turns syrupy, stirring three or four times with a wooden spoon.

3 Meanwhile, peel the papayas, remove the centre seeds and coarsely chop the flesh. Add to the bowl with the tamarind, nutmeg and salt. Still uncovered, cook on Medium until the chutney thickens to a jam-like consistency, stirring three or four times.

4 Stir in the remaining ingredients.

5 Allow to cool to lukewarm, then remove the tamarind seeds with a draining spoon. Ladle the chutney into warmed jars, top with paper discs and leave until cold.

6 Cover with non-metallic lids or cellophane and label the jars.

Curried Mango Chutney

If you happen to live near a fruit and vegetable market, mangoes are often sold off inexpensively at the end of the day, especially at weekends, giving you the perfect excuse to make this spicy, fairly hot, Eastern chutney without spending a fortune.

makes 750 g/1¾ lb/2 small jars

1 long red chilli, about 7.5 cm/3 in

1 long green chilli, about 7.5 cm/3 in

4 shallots, halved

3 garlic cloves

5 medium just-ripe mangoes

10 ml/2 tsp salt

30 ml/2 tbsp mild curry powder

175 ml/6 fl oz/¾ cup lemon juice

175 g/6 oz/¾ cup golden granulated sugar

1 Leave the seeds in the chillies if you want the chutney to be on the hot side; otherwise slit each one, open up and remove and discard the seeds. Coarsely grind the chillies, shallots and garlic in a food processor or finely chop by hand.

2 Peel the mangoes and cut the flesh away from stones (pits) in strips or slices. Coarsely chop the flesh.

3 Put all the ingredients in a 3 litre/5 pt/12½ cup capacity bowl. Leave uncovered and cook on Full (750–800w) for 35–40 minutes until the chutney thickens to a jam-like consistency, stirring three or four times with a wooden spoon.

4 Allow to cool to lukewarm, then ladle into warmed jars, top with paper discs and leave until cold.

5 Cover with non-metallic lids or cellophane and label the jars.

Pineapple and Pear Chutney with Raisins

A festive winter chutney with a natural affinity to Christmas meats and poultry.

makes 1 kg/2¼ lb/2 jars

1 medium pineapple, peeled and eyes removed

225 g/8 oz onions, cut into eighths

2 garlic cloves, halved

60 ml/4 tbsp water

15 ml/1 tbsp salt

100 g/4 oz/⅔ cup raisins

100 g/4 oz/⅔ cup dried pears, snipped into small pieces

15 ml/1 tbsp ground ginger

5 ml/1 tsp ground cinnamon

5 ml/1 tsp ground allspice

Grated (shredded) zest of 1 medium lemon

225 g/8 oz/1 cup soft light brown sugar

350 ml/12 fl oz/1⅓ cups brown malt vinegar

1 Slice the pineapple, then cut each slice into six wedges. Put into a food processor with the onions and garlic and grind coarsely.

2 Scrape into a 4 litre/7 pt/17½ cup capacity bowl and stir in the water and salt. Leave uncovered and cook on Full (750–800w) for 5 minutes.

3 Add all the remaining ingredients and stir well. Leave uncovered and continue to cook on Full for 35–40 minutes until the chutney thickens to a jam-like consistency, stirring four or five times with a wooden spoon. If the chutney is too runny, cook for an extra 5–10 minutes until it reaches the desired thickness.

4 Allow to cool to lukewarm, then ladle into warmed jars, top with paper discs and leave until cold.

5 Cover with non-metallic lids or cellophane and label the jars.

Rhubarb and Pear Chutney with Apricots

A smart one for cold meats and rich poultry such as duck and goose, this chutney also goes well with game and pork pies, sausages and anything barbecued. The Japanese shichimi seasoning gives a flavour lift to the whole thing, making the chutney curiously Asiatic.

makes 1.25 kg/2½ lb/2 large jars

100 g/4 oz/⅔ cup dried apricots
Boiling water
100 g/4 oz rhubarb, trimmed and cut into small chunks
350 g/12 oz pears, peeled, cored and quartered
3 garlic cloves
450 ml/¾ pt/2 cups colourless distilled malt vinegar
1 cinnamon stick
10 ml/2 tsp shichimi seasoning
10 ml/2 tsp ready-prepared tamarind pulp
10–15 ml/2–3 tsp salt
225 g/8 oz/1 cup golden granulated sugar

1 Put the apricots into a bowl, cover with boiling water and cook, uncovered, on Full (750–800w) for 4 minutes. Leave to cool, then drain.

2 Put the apricots, rhubarb, pears and garlic in a food processor and coarsely chop.

3 Transfer to a 4 litre/7 pt/17½ cup capacity bowl with all the remaining ingredients. Leave uncovered and cook on Full for 30–40 minutes until the chutney thickens to a jam-like consistency, stirring four times with a wooden spoon.

4 Allow to cool to lukewarm, remove the cinnamon stick, then ladle into warmed jars, top with paper discs and leave until cold.

5 Cover with non-metallic lids or cellophane and label the jars.

Green Tomato Chutney

Tomatoes from a neighbour's garden produced this turn-of-the-century-style chutney in a stunning shade of green and with a most pleasing flavour.

makes 900 g/2 lb/2 jars

700 g/1½ lb green tomatoes, quartered

2 medium onions, about 225 g/8 oz, quartered

3 garlic cloves, halved

Finely grated peel and juice of 1 medium lemon

2 whole fresh plump green chillies

175 ml/6 fl oz/¾ cup colourless distilled malt vinegar

225 g/8 oz/1 cup granulated sugar

1.5 ml/½ tsp dried basil

15 ml/1 tbsp mixed pickling spice, securely twisted in a coffee filter paper bag

1 Coarsely chop the tomatoes, onions and garlic in a food processor.

2 Transfer to a 2.25 litre/4 pt/10 cup capacity bowl with all the remaining ingredients including the bag of spice. Leave uncovered and cook on Full (750–800w) for about 35 minutes until the chutney thickens to a jam-like consistency, stirring three or four times with a wooden spoon.

3 Allow to cool to lukewarm, then remove the bag of spices, ladle into warmed jars and top with paper discs. Leave until cold.

4 Cover with non-metallic lids or cellophane and label the jars.

Hot Tomato Chutney

Nothing better for burgers, sausages and all things Mexican, this is a spiced and colourful chutney.

makes 1.5 kg/3 lb/3 jars

2 medium onions, cut into chunks
1 long red chilli, about 8 cm/3 in, split and seeded
225 g/8 oz red (bell) peppers, halved and seeded
225 g/8 oz cooking (tart) apples, peeled, cored and quartered
2 garlic cloves, halved
750 g/1¾ lb ripe tomatoes, skinned
150 ml/¼ pt/⅔ cup malt vinegar
150 ml/¼ pt/⅔ cup lemon juice
225 g/8 oz/1 cup soft light brown sugar
150 ml/¼ pt tomato purée (paste)
10–20 ml/2–4 tsp chilli powder
10 ml/2 tsp sweet paprika
5 ml/1 tsp mustard powder
15 ml/1 tbsp salt

1 Put the onions, chilli, peppers, apples and garlic in a food processor and coarsely chop. Pulse in the tomatoes. Transfer to a 4 litre/7 pt/17½ cup capacity bowl and add all the remaining ingredients.

2 Leave uncovered and cook on Medium (550w) for 40 minutes, stirring four or five times with a wooden spoon.

3 Leave to rest for 15 minutes, then continue to cook on Medium for a further 15 minutes until the chutney reaches a jam-like consistency, stirring twice.

4 Allow to cool to lukewarm, then ladle into warmed jars, top with paper discs and leave until cold.

5 Cover with non-metallic lids or cellophane and label the jars.

Salsas and Relishes

Modern versions of pickles, salsas – Spanish for sauce – and relishes have spread from North and Central America and tend to be crisp, juicy and full-flavoured, companionable with almost everything from barbecued foods, egg dishes and cold pies to cheese, cold meats, poultry, smoked fish and sandwiches.

Bean and Vegetable Salsa

Based on a salsa brought to me by friends from America, this is easy to make, tastes chirpy and keeps well in the fridge.

makes 750 g/1¾ lb/2 small jars

150 g/5 oz head of fennel, trimmed and sliced

75 g/3 oz celery, cut into chunks

1 large onion, about 175 g/6 oz, cut into chunks

400 g/14 oz/1 large can of baked beans in tomato sauce

45 ml/3 tbsp tomato ketchup (catsup)

15 ml/1 tbsp Worcestershire sauce

5 ml/1 tsp jalapeño sauce

5 ml/1 tsp garlic paste

30 ml/2 tbsp light-coloured distilled malt vinegar

1.5–5 ml/¼–1 tsp chilli sauce (optional)

1 Put all the ingredients in a food processor, including the chilli sauce if you like a hotter flavour, and chop fairly finely.

2 Transfer to a 2.25 litre/4 pt/10 cup capacity bowl and cook on Full (750–800w) for 6 minutes.

3 Allow to cool to lukewarm, then ladle into warmed jars, top with paper discs and leave until cold.

4 Cover with non-metallic lids or cellophane and label the jars.

5 Store in the fridge for up to two months.

Cool Green Cucumber Salsa

Because cucumbers and fresh mint read summer, this is a delicious salsa to have on hand for cold food and sandwiches. It is also wonderful served with barbecued meats, sausages and poultry.

makes 900 g/2 lb/2 jars

700 g/1½ lb cucumbers, peeled and thickly sliced

1 green (bell) pepper, about 100 g/4 oz, seeded and cut into strips

2 celery sticks, cut into chunks

2 crisp, green eating (dessert) apples, such as Granny Smith, about 225 g/8 oz, peeled, cored and quartered

1 large onion, about 225 g/8 oz, cut into chunks

2 garlic cloves, sliced

120 ml/4 fl oz/½ cup mint leaves

75 ml/5 tbsp colourless distilled malt vinegar

150 g/5 oz/⅔ cup granulated sugar

15 ml/1 tbsp jalapeño sauce

10 ml/2 tsp salt

1 Put the cucumber, pepper, celery, apples, onion, garlic and mint into a food processor and chop fairly finely, then transfer to a 3 litre/5 pt/12½ cup capacity bowl.

2 Leave uncovered and cook on Medium (550w) for 12 minutes, stirring twice with a wooden spoon.

3 Add the remaining ingredients and continue to cook, uncovered, for 30–35 minutes until the salsa thickens to an almost jam-like consistency, stirring three or four times.

4 Allow to cool to lukewarm, then ladle into warmed jars, top with paper discs and leave until cold.

5 Cover with non-metallic lids or cellophane and label the jars.

6 Store in the fridge for up to two months.

Mild Mango Salsa

An absolute gem for anyone with a yen for real exotica, this has the wonderful sweet flavour of mango that complements all kinds of meats.

makes 700 g/1½ lb/2 small jars

225 g/8 oz onions, cut into chunks

75 g/3 oz fresh root ginger, peeled and thinly sliced

3 garlic cloves, sliced

30 ml/2 tbsp lemon juice

5–7.5 ml/1–1½ tsp salt

150 ml/¼ pt/⅔ cup passata (sieved tomatoes)

2 medium ripe mangoes

1.5–5 ml/¼–1 tsp cayenne

5 ml/1 tsp ground coriander (cilantro)

1 Put the onions, ginger and garlic in a food processor and chop fairly finely. Transfer to a 2.25 litre/4 pt/10 cup capacity bowl and add the lemon juice, salt to taste and the passata.

2 Cook, uncovered, on Full (750–800w) for 4 minutes, stirring once.

3 Peel the mangoes, cut the flesh away from the stones (pits) and dice the flesh. Stir into the hot ingredients with cayenne to taste and the coriander. Stir well to mix.

4 Leave to cool completely, then ladle into jars, top with paper discs and lids or cellophane and label the jars.

5 Store in the fridge for up to two months.

Papaya Salsa

A stingingly hot and spicy salsa for all things Mexican, for ribs and burgers and for barbecued chicken. See photograph opposite page 144.

makes 750 g/1½ lb/2 small jars

> 1 red (bell) pepper, about 100 g/4 oz, seeded and cut into chunks
>
> 1 green (bell) pepper, about 100 g/4 oz, seeded and cut into chunks
>
> 1 large onion, cut into chunks
>
> 2 garlic cloves, sliced
>
> 60 ml/4 tbsp boiling water
>
> 7.5 ml/1½ tsp salt
>
> 1 large or 2 medium papaya, about 350 g/12 oz
>
> 350 g/12 oz tomatoes, skinned and chopped
>
> 20 ml/4 tsp shop-bought bottled green peppercorns in brine, well-drained
>
> 30 ml/2 tbsp malt vinegar
>
> 45 ml/3 tbsp passata (sieved tomatoes)

1 Put the peppers, onion and garlic in a food processor and chop fairly finely. Transfer to a 3.5 litre/6 pt/15 cup capacity bowl and add the boiling water and salt. Leave uncovered and cook on Full (750–800w) for 6 minutes.

2 Meanwhile, peel the papaya, halve each one and remove and discard the inside dark brown seeds, then chop the flesh. Add to the bowl with the remaining ingredients.

3 Leave uncovered and cook on Full for 12 minutes, stirring three times.

4 Allow to cool to lukewarm, then ladle into warmed jars, top with paper discs. and leave until cold.

5 Cover with non-metallic lids or cellophane and label the jars.

6 Store in a cool, dark place or in the fridge for up to two months.

Two-pepper Tomato Salsa with Lime

A gazpacho taste-alike with a hot kick, perfect to accompany grilled (broiled) and barbecued meats and anything with a Mexican flavour. Wash your hands and utensils thoroughly after preparing chillies as the oils will irritate the eyes or delicate skin. Rub a little olive oil into your hands before touching them or wear plastic gloves to prevent the oil lingering on your hands.

makes 1 kg/2¼ lb/2 jars

350 g/12 oz red (bell) peppers
1 large onion, about 225 g/8 oz, thickly sliced
1 x 7.5 cm/3 in red chilli, slit and seeded
1 x 5 cm/2 in green chilli, slit and seeded
45 ml/3 tbsp sun-dried tomato paste
3 garlic cloves, halved
10 ml/2 tsp salt
15 ml/1 tbsp caster (superfine) sugar
Juice of 1 lime
700 g/1½ lb ripe tomatoes, skinned

1 Put the peppers in a plastic food bag and tie the bag loosely at the top, leaving a small gap to prevent the bag swelling and popping. (Do NOT use a metal twist-tie.) Soften the peppers by cooking on Full (750–800w) for 8 minutes, turning the bag over twice.

2 Leave the peppers in the bag to cool for 30 minutes, then rinse under cold water, slit open and remove the fibres and seeds. Cut the flesh into wide strips. Put the pepper flesh, onion, chillies, tomato paste, garlic, salt, sugar and lime juice in a food processor and chop fairly finely, then pulse in the tomatoes.

3 Transfer to a 3 litre/5 pt/12½ cup bowl and cook on Full (750–800w) for 5 minutes to mature the flavours.

4 Allow to cool to lukewarm, then ladle into warmed jars, top with paper discs and leave until cold.

5 Cover with non-metallic lids or cellophane and label the jars.

6 Store in the fridge for up to two months.

Crispy Carrot and Coriander Relish

A rough-cast, sweet-sour pickle-like condiment with a bitey texture and up-to-the-minute flavour. It contrasts beautifully with white cheeses from Greece, India's pale yellow *paneer,* and Cheddar or Stilton when it's packed into crusty bread for a ploughman's. It's also happy enough with curries. The dried and sweetened cranberries are available at major supermarkets in winter. See photograph overleaf from page 97.

makes 1.25 kg/2½ lb/2 large jars

450 g/1 lb carrots, thickly sliced
4 garlic cloves, halved
350 g/12 oz young leeks, sliced lengthways and cut into chunks
100 g/4 oz fresh coriander (cilantro)
10 ml/2 tsp yellow mustard seeds
1.5 ml/¼ tsp grated nutmeg
75 g/3 oz/½ cup dried sweetened cranberries OR raisins
5 ml/1 tsp Tabasco sauce
10 ml/2 tsp salt
450 ml/¾ pt/2 cups colourless distilled malt vinegar
350 g/12 oz/1½ cups granulated sugar
15 ml/1 tbsp lemon juice

1 Put the carrots, garlic, leeks and coriander in a food processor and process until finely chopped. Scrape into a 4 litre/7 pt/17½ cup capacity bowl and stir in all the remaining ingredients except the sugar and lemon juice.

2 Leave uncovered and cook on Full (750–800w) for 20 minutes, stirring two or three times with a wooden spoon.

3 Thoroughly stir in the sugar.

4 Continue to cook on Full, uncovered, for a further 30 minutes or until the relish is a dark colour and minimal liquid remains, stirring several times.

5 Stir in the lemon juice and adjust the salt to taste, then ladle into warmed jars, top with paper discs and leave until cold.

6 Cover with non-metallic lids or cellophane and label the jars.

7 Store in a cool, dark place for up to two months.

Cucumber and Piccalilli Relish

A prize relish for grilled (broiled) food and barbecues of both meat and fish. Cassia bark is available from delicatessens and oriental shops.

makes 450 g/1 lb/1 jar

900 g/2 lb cucumbers, peeled and finely grated (shredded)

4 fresh tamarind

150 ml/¼ pt/⅔ cup colourless distilled malt vinegar

150 ml/¼ pt/⅔ cup boiling water

75 g/3 oz/⅓ cup granulated sugar

15 ml/1 tbsp salt

5 ml/1 tsp turmeric

15 ml/1 tbsp mixed pickling spice

5 cm/2 in piece of cassia bark

2 bay leaves

1 sprig of dried thyme

10 ml/2 tsp cornflour (cornstarch)

15 ml/1 tbsp cold water

1 Strain the cucumbers through a fine mesh sieve (strainer) lined with an opened-out paper coffee filter bag until almost dry, stirring occasionally.

2 Remove and discard the brittle shells and inside strings from the tamarind, then remove the seeds. Put the cucumber, tamarind, vinegar, boiling water, sugar, salt and turmeric in a 3 litre/5 pt/12½ cup capacity bowl.

3 Tie the pickling spice, cassia, bay leaves and thyme in a piece of muslin (cheesecloth) or twist securely in a large paper coffee filter bag. Add to the bowl and cook, uncovered, on Full (750–800w) for 5 minutes.

4 Mix the cornflour to a smooth paste with the cold water and stir into the cucumber mixture. Leave uncovered and continue to cook on Medium (550w) for 12 minutes until slightly thickened, stirring gently two or three times with a wooden spoon.

5 Allow to cool to lukewarm, then ladle into warmed jars, top with paper discs and leave until cold.

6 Cover with non-metallic lids or cellophane and label the jars. Store in a cool, dark place and eat within three to four weeks.

Cucumber and Celery Relish

Striking to look at and surprisingly strong, this relish is super with cheeses of all kinds. It requires minimal cooking so it's quick and easy to create.

makes 1.5 kg/3 lb/3 jars

2 large cucumbers, about 900 g/2 lb
350 g/12 oz onions, cut into chunks
225 g/8 oz celery sticks, cut into chunks
150 ml/¼ pt/⅔ cup boiling water
150 g/5 oz/⅔ cup granulated sugar
175 ml/6 fl oz/¾ cup colourless distilled malt vinegar
10 ml/2 tsp celery salt
5 ml/1 tsp plain salt
1 cinnamon stick, broken into 3 pieces
3 bay leaves
3 whole cloves

1 Peel the cucumbers, halve lengthways, then use a teaspoon to scoop out and discard the seeds. Slice the cucumber shells thinly, place in a colander and leave to drain while preparing the rest of the ingredients.

2 Chop the onion and celery either by hand or in a food processor. Put in a 4 litre/7 pt/17½ cup capacity bowl and add the boiling water. Leave uncovered and cook on Full (750–800w) for 8 minutes.

3 Stir in all the remaining ingredients including the cucumber slices.

4 Allow to cool to lukewarm, then ladle into warmed jars, top with paper discs and leave until cold.

5 Cover with non-metallic lids or cellophane and label the jars.

6 Store in the fridge for about two weeks.

Red Mediterranean Tomato Relish

Piquant and trendy, this relish can be treated as a condiment or used as a sauce base for spaghetti Bolognese and chilli con carne. See photograph opposite.

makes 700 g/1½ lb/2 small jars

1 medium red (bell) pepper, halved and seeded
1 medium yellow (bell) pepper, halved and seeded
1 celery stick, cut into chunks
1 large onion, about 225 g/8 oz, cut into chunks
2 garlic cloves, sliced
450 g/1 lb ripe tomatoes, skinned
60 ml/4 tbsp hot water
5 ml/1 tsp celery salt
5 ml/1 tsp salt
30 ml/2 tbsp balsamic vinegar
30 ml/2 tbsp colourless distilled malt vinegar
100 g/4 oz/½ cup granulated sugar
2 dried bird's eye chillies
15 ml/1 tbsp lemon juice

1 Put the peppers, celery, onion and garlic in a food processor and chop fairly finely. Pulse in the tomatoes. Transfer to a 3 litre/5 pt/12½ cup capacity bowl with all the remaining ingredients.

2 Leave uncovered and cook on Medium (550w) for 35–40 minutes until the mixture is thick and much of the liquid has evaporated, stirring three or four times with a wooden spoon.

3 Allow to cool to lukewarm, then ladle into warmed jars, top with paper discs and leave until cold.

4 Cover with non-metallic lids or cellophane and label the jars.

5 Store in the fridge for up to six weeks.

Opposite: *Red Mediterranean Tomato Relish and Papaya Salsa (page 139)*

Pickles

There is more to pickles than onions and eggs, and this section highlights variations on a theme featuring not only pickled vegetables but also fruits such as damsons and tomatoes.

Opposite: *Lemon and Persimmon Pickle (page 148)*

Sweet and Sour Red Cabbage Pickle

With a slightly oriental flavour to it, this pickle is a variation of traditional pickled red cabbage, but the mix of spices works exceptionally well and the pickle seems to go enthusiastically with cold salads, pork pies, sausages and ham. If you wear rubber gloves while preparing the cabbage, it will prevent the juices staining your hands. See photograph overleaf from page 97.

makes 1.25 kg/2½ lb/2 large jars

900 g/2 lb head of red cabbage, quartered and finely shredded
45 ml/3 tbsp salt
300 ml/½ pt/1¼ cups rice vinegar
10 ml/2 tsp five-spice powder
2.5 ml/½ tsp grated nutmeg
3 garlic cloves, peeled and crushed
100 g/4 oz/½ cup soft light brown sugar

1 Put the cabbage in a 4 litre/7 pt/17½ cup capacity bowl and toss thoroughly with the salt. Cover with a plate or lid and leave to stand for 24 hours.

2 Rinse the cabbage in a colander under cold running water, then leave to drain.

3 Put all the remaining ingredients in the bowl, leave uncovered and cook on Full (750–800w) for 5 minutes, stirring once.

4 Stir in the cabbage and, still uncovered, cook on Full for 4 minutes. Toss gently with two spoons or spatulas until thoroughly mixed.

5 Spoon into warmed jars, top with paper discs and leave until cold.

6 Cover with non-metallic lids or cellophane and label the jars.

7 Store in a cool, dark place for up to three months.

Mixed Vegetable Pickle

A cool, crisp pickle that is healthy and bright. You can serve this with fish or light meats.

makes 1.5 kg/3 lb/3 jars

450 g/1 lb head of white cabbage, cut into chunks

225 g/8 oz carrots, cut into chunks

225 g/8 oz green (bell) peppers, seeded and cut into chunks

3 medium celery sticks, about 100 g/4 oz, cut into chunks

350 g/12 oz onions, quartered

1 large cucumber, about 350 g/12 oz, thickly sliced

60 ml/4 tbsp salt

300 ml/½ pt/1¼ cups colourless distilled malt vinegar

3 garlic cloves, crushed

150 g/5 oz/⅔ cup granulated sugar

10–15 ml/2–3 tsp Thai seven-spice seasoning

1 Put the cabbage, carrots, peppers, celery, onions and cucumber in a food processor and chop fairly finely. Transfer to a 4 litre/7 pt/17½ cup capacity bowl. Toss thoroughly with the salt, cover with a plate or lid and leave to stand for 24 hours.

2 Tip into a colander and rinse under cold running water, then leave to drain.

3 Put all the remaining ingredients in the bowl, leave uncovered and cook on Full (750 800w) for 5 minutes, stirring once.

4 Stir in the drained vegetables, mixing them in well.

5 Still uncovered, cook on Full for a further 7 minutes.

6 Toss gently with two spoons or spatulas until thoroughly mixed, then spoon into warmed jars, top with paper discs and leave until cold.

7 Cover with non-metallic lids or cellophane and label the jars.

8 Store in a cool, dark place for up to three months.

Lemon and Persimmon Pickle

A lively, golden amber-coloured and startlingly fresh-tasting off-beat pickle. It is quite special with oriental foods, poultry, sausages, roast pork and strong blue cheeses, and a spoon or two can be stirred into thick yoghurt to make a unique dip or salad dressing. See photograph opposite page 145.

makes 750 g/1½ lb/2 small jars

30 ml/2 tbsp mixed pickling spice

3–4 large persimmons, about 450 g/1 lb in total, quartered and stoned (pitted)

3 medium lemons, about 250 g/9 oz, topped, tailed and sliced

225 g/8 oz onions, quartered

1 garlic clove, sliced

1 x 15 g/1 x ½ oz red chilli, split and seeded

30 ml/2 tbsp water

225 g/8 oz/1 cup granulated sugar

300 ml/½ pt/1¼ cups colourless distilled malt vinegar

1 Tip the spice into a coffee filter paper bag and close up to form a small package. Set aside.

2 Put the persimmons, lemons, onions, garlic and chilli in a food processor and chop coarsely. Scrape into a 3 litre/5 pt/12½ cup capacity bowl.

3 Cook, uncovered, on Full (750–800w) for 5 minutes.

4 Stir well, then stir in all the remaining ingredients and add the bag of spice.

5 Leave uncovered, and cook on Full for 40–45 minutes, stirring four or five times.

6 Allow to cool to lukewarm, discard the bag of spice, then ladle into warmed jars, top with paper discs and leave until cold.

7 Cover with non-metallic lids or cellophane and label the jars.

8 Store in the fridge for up to a month.

Indian-style Hot Lime Chutney Pickle

A pickle with kick, this recipe economically uses the lemon and lime pulp left from the Clear Lemon and Lime Jelly Marmalade on page 74 and turns out hot, pungent and slightly bitter, marvellous with tandooris and Indian breads. A few spoonfuls stirred into thick yoghurt makes a stylish dip with baby popadoms. You can buy small jars of ginger in oil from supermarkets and delicatessens.

makes 1 kg/2¼ lb/2 jars

Pulp from Clear Lemon and Lime Jelly Marmalade (see page 74)

75 g/3 oz/²⁄₃ cup granulated sugar

175 ml/6 fl oz/³⁄₄ cup groundnut (peanut) or corn oil

10 ml/2 tsp mustard powder

10 ml/2 tsp ground cumin

10 ml/2 tsp chilli powder

10 ml/2 tsp paprika

12.5 ml/2½ tsp bottled fresh ginger in soya bean oil

5 ml/1 tsp garam masala

5 ml/1 tsp turmeric

4 garlic cloves, crushed

1 Put all the ingredients in a 2.25 litre/4 pt/10 cup capacity bowl. Leave uncovered and cook on Full (750–800w) for 10 minutes, stirring twice with a wooden spoon.

2 Allow to cool to lukewarm, then ladle into warmed jars, top with paper discs and leave until cold.

3 Cover with lids or cellophane and label the jars.

4 Store in the fridge for up to three weeks.

Mustard Pickled Cucumber Chunks

Cheerfully yellow cucumber pickles, these team well with anything and everything cold.

makes 1 kg/2¼ lb/2 jars

700 g/1½ lb cucumbers, peeled

300 ml/½ pt/1¼ cup colourless distilled malt vinegar

150 ml/¼ pt/⅔ cup water

65 g/2½ oz granulated sugar

15 ml/1 tbsp pickling spice

2 garlic cloves, crushed

15 ml/1 tbsp salt

2.5 ml/½ tsp mustard powder

2.5 ml/½ tsp turmeric

1 Cut the cucumbers into 9 cm/3½ in chunks, then cut each chunk downwards into four strips.

2 Pour the vinegar into a 3 litre/5 pt/12½ cup capacity bowl and stir in all the remaining ingredients except the cucumber.

3 Leave uncovered and cook on Full (750–800w) for 5 minutes, stirring three times with a wooden spoon.

4 Stir in the cucumber thoroughly. Cover loosely and leave until cold.

5 Spoon into jars, making sure the vinegar liquid comes to the top of the jars. Cover with non-metallic lids or cellophane and label the jars.

6 Store in the fridge to retain crispness and eat within two weeks.

Pickled Cucumber and Red Onion Wafers

Like a tumble of autumn (fall) leaves, these flamboyant and vividly coloured cucumber pickles look dark and dramatic in their jars. This recipe is based on North American bread and butter pickles, used profusely for sandwiches, and their tawny character here is brought about by using burgundy-skinned red onions. Use it also as a tangy sweet-sharp condiment to go with meat, rich fish, cheese and Asian and Indian specialities.

makes about 1.5 kg/3 lb/3 jars

750 g /1½ lb cucumbers
2 medium–large red onions, 225 g/8 oz in total, very thinly sliced into rings
275 ml/9 fl oz /1⅛ cup colourless distilled malt vinegar
175 g/6 oz/¾ cup caster (superfine) sugar
15 ml/1 tbsp mixed pickling spice
15 ml/1 tbsp salt
2.5 ml/½ tsp mustard powder
2.5 ml/½ tsp turmeric
4 generous sprigs of fresh coriander (cilantro)

1 Shave wafer-thin slices off the unpeeled cucumber and place in a colander with the onion rings. Leave to drain for 30 minutes.

2 Pour the vinegar into a 4 litre/7 pt/17½ cup capacity bowl and stir in all the remaining ingredients except the cucumber, onion and coriander. Leave uncovered and cook on Full (750–800w) for 5 minutes.

3 Stir in the cucumber, onion and coriander. Cook on Full for 5 minutes, still uncovered, stirring three times.

4 Allow to cool to lukewarm, then ladle into warmed jars, top with paper discs and leave until cold.

5 Cover with non-metallic lids or cellophane and label the jars.

6 Store in the fridge to retain crispness for up to four weeks.

Pickled Eggs

Pub food at home! Because the eggs are pickled in dark instead of colourless vinegar, they look as though they've been left in their original brown shells, more appetising and appealing by far than those stark white eggs you find in jars in bars and supermarkets.

makes 12

12 large eggs
900 ml/1½ pt/3¾ cups Spiced Pickling Vinegar (see page 162)

1 Place the eggs in a large pan of cold water, bring to the boil, then boil for 9 minutes.

2 Drain well, rinse in cold water, then cover with cold water. Crack each egg lightly, wipe dry and leave until cold, then remove the shells.

3 Put the eggs in a 1.75 litre/3 pt/7½ cup capacity jar with a wide neck.

4 Pour the vinegar into a 1.2 litre/2 pt/5 cup capacity measuring jug and heat on Full (750–800w) for 7 minutes.

5 Pour over the eggs, then leave until cold.

6 Cover the jar with a double thickness of microwave wrap (plastic wrap), then cover with a non-metallic lid or cellophane and label the jar.

7 Store in a cool, dark place for up to five months.

Pickled Button Mushrooms

Always useful as a condiment to serve with poultry, fish and vegetarian meals, these mushrooms keep well in the cool but the flavour becomes stronger as the weeks go by, so they are best eaten within three months. Using frozen mushrooms saves time and preparation, though you can use fresh mushrooms if you wish. Wood-smoked salt is available from speciality food shops and some supermarkets.

makes 1 kg/2¼ lb/2 jars

450 g/1 lb frozen button mushrooms
450 ml/¾ pt/1½ cups light-coloured seasoned pickling vinegar
60 ml/4 tbsp granulated sugar
15 ml/1 tbsp salt, preferably wood-smoked

1 Tip the mushrooms into a 1 litre/1¾ pt/4¼ cup capacity jar.

2 Put the remaining ingredients in a 1.2 litre/2 pt/5 cup capacity bowl and cook, uncovered, on Full (750–800w) for 5 minutes, stirring occasionally with a wooden spoon, until the sugar has dissolved. Ladle into the jar of mushrooms and leave until cold.

3 Top with a paper disc, then cover with a non-metallic lid or cellophane and label the jars.

4 Store in a cool, dark place for up to three months.

Asian-style Pickled Baby Sweetcorn

Hot, spicy, aromatic and addictive, sweetcorn (corn) is an absolute must with Far Eastern food and curries. You can adjust the number of chillies you use to suit your own taste. The seasoned rice vinegar dressing can be found in major supermarkets but you can also use unseasoned rice vinegar.

makes 1 kg/2¼ lb/2 jars

550 g/1¼ lb frozen baby sweetcorn (corn) cobs
20 fresh coriander (cilantro) leaves
750 ml/1¼ pts/3 cups seasoned rice vinegar dressing
60 ml/4 tbsp granulated sugar
5 ml/1 tsp salt
2 garlic cloves, thinly sliced
4–8 fresh or dried bird's eye chillies
2 stems of lemon grass, trimmed and thinly sliced

1 Put the sweetcorn in one large 1.2 litre/2 pt/5 cup capacity jar or two smaller jars with all but four of the coriander leaves.

2 Put the remaining ingredients in a 1.75 litre/3 pt/7½ cup capacity bowl and cook, uncovered, on Full (750–800w) for 7 minutes until the sugar has dissolved, stirring twice with a wooden spoon.

3 Slowly spoon the mixture over the sweetcorn, place the reserved coriander leaves on top and leave until cold.

4 Cover with a paper disc, then with a non-metallic lid or cellophane and label the jars.

5 Store in a cool, dark place for up to three months.

Pickled Aubergines

These fleshy little aubergines (eggplants) are typically Turkish and Greek, superb in a Middle Eastern salad or as a side dish with kebabs and roasted lamb. It is important that you use the small, round or oval aubergines that are available in major supermarkets or in Middle Eastern and Indian stores.

makes 1.25 kg/2½ lb/2 large jars

750 g/1¾ lb small round or oval aubergines
6–8 fresh or dried bird's eye chillies
About 450 ml/¾ pt/2 cups Spiced Pickling Vinegar (page 162)

1 Arrange the aubergines round the edge of two plates. Prick lightly all over with a fork and cook each plate of aubergines individually on Full (750–800w) for about 6 minutes until soft.

2 Drop the aubergines into the jars with the whole chillies and top up with cold spiced vinegar.

3 Leave until cold, then top with a paper disc and cover with a non-metallic lid or cellophane.

4 Label and store in the dark for up to three months.

Pickled Green Tomatoes

makes 1.25 kg/2½ lb/2 large jars

These sharpish tomatoes are classically British from a bygone age, designed to be eaten with Cheddar and Stilton cheeses, Melton Mowbray pie, Cornish pasties, black pudding and Cumberland sausages. Prepare as for Pickled Aubergines, but substitute whole green tomatoes for the aubergines and use hot spiced vinegar instead of cold.

Pickled Damsons

A real golden oldie, a taste from the past, these damsons, which are pickled whole and still with their stones (pits), are strikingly flavoured and dark, dark red. They taste blissful with pork, gammon and game. For a softer and more purée-like fruit, cook the damsons for an extra 3–4 minutes.

makes 700 g/1½ lb/2 small jars

450 g/1 lb damsons
225 g/8 oz/1 cup granulated sugar
150 ml/¼ pt/⅔ cup colourless distilled malt vinegar
6 whole cloves
1 cinnamon stick
6 whole allspice
15 ml/1 tsp Sechuan pepper
2.5 ml/½ tsp fennel seeds
5 ml/1 tsp salt

1 Prick the damsons all over with a fork and set aside.

2 Put all the remaining ingredients in a 3 litre/5 pt/12½ cup capacity bowl. Leave uncovered and cook on Full (750–800w) for 5 minutes, stirring twice with a wooden spoon.

3 Stir in the damsons and continue to cook on Full for a further 3–4 minutes until the damsons just begin to split.

4 Allow to cool to lukewarm, then ladle into jars, top with paper discs and leave until cold.

5 Cover with non-metallic lids or cellophane and label the jars.

6 Store in a cool, dark place or the fruit will lose its colour. Keep for up to six months.

Pickled Mangoes

Layers of flavour come across in this almost mystic-tasting luxury pickle, which stays bright mustard yellow and teams perfectly with strong or mild curries, and fried (sautéed) foods generally.

makes 900 g/2 lb/2 jars

1.5 kg/3 lb just-ripe mangoes
300 ml/½ pt/1¼ cups colourless distilled malt vinegar
175 g/6 oz/¾ cup granulated sugar
10 ml/2 tsp ground ginger
10 ml/2 tsp salt

1 Peel the mangoes, cut the flesh away from the stones (pits), then dice the flesh. Spoon into a 900 ml/1½ pt/3¾ cup jar.

2 Put the remaining ingredients in a 1.5 litre/2½ pt/6 cup capacity bowl. Leave uncovered and cook on Full (750–800w) for 4–5 minutes until the sugar has dissolved, stirring once with a wooden spoon. Leave until cold.

3 Spoon the syrup over the mangoes, top with a paper disc, then cover with a non-metallic lid or cellophane and label the jars.

4 Store in a cool, dark place for up to four months.

Pickled Pears

An elegant and sophisticated, deep amber pickle that keeps well and tastes glorious. It makes the perfect partner for lamb, gammon and grilled (broiled) tuna and, for an exceptional dessert, serve it with vanilla ice cream and use any leftover vinegary syrup in the salad dressing.

makes 900 g/2 lb/2 jars

450 g/1 lb/2 cups golden granulated sugar
300 ml/½ pt/1¼ cups raspberry vinegar
5 ml/1 tsp ground allspice
5 ml/1 tsp ground ginger
6 just-ripe pears, such as Conference
2 cinnamon sticks
4 whole cloves

1 Put all the ingredients except the pears, cinnamon sticks and cloves in a 3 litre/ 5 pt/12½ cup capacity bowl. Leave uncovered and cook on Medium (550w) for 9 minutes, stirring twice with a wooden spoon.

2 Meanwhile peel, core and quarter the pears. Add to the hot vinegar and sugar mix. Leave uncovered and cook on Medium for 10–12 minutes until the pears are softish and beginning to look transparent.

3 Transfer the pears to a 900 ml/1½ pt/3¾ cup capacity jar, or two smaller jars, and add the cinnamon sticks and cloves.

4 Cook the remaining vinegar mixture, uncovered, on Medium for about 15 minutes until it thickens to a syrupy consistency. Leave until cold.

5 Spoon the syrup over the pears, reserving a small amount for topping up as the fruit will absorb the vinegary syrup over the following 24 hours.

6 Add the reserved vinegar, top with a paper disc, then cover with a non-metallic lid or cellophane and label the jar.

7 Store in a cool, dark place for up to six months.

Flavoured Vinegars

Ideal for pickles, chutneys, East-West dressings and cooking in general, these vinegars are one step up in quality from the ones you can buy and each has its own individuality and character, providing you with a choice of flavours, colours and even medicinal benefits.

Fruit Vinegar

History revisited! The basis for this recipe came from a 1920s cook book, where it was described as a remedy for coughs when taken neat and a cooling and refreshing long drink for hot summer days if mixed with iced soda water. Adapted for the microwave, this particular vinegar has become an essential basic in my home. A few teaspoonfuls stirred into a tumbler of cold or hot water eases a dry, tickly throat almost immediately – the author knew her alternative medicine all those years ago – and it's blissfully cooling splashed with fizzy water or lemonade, and when mixed with oil makes a modern salad dressing. It appears to have indefinite keeping qualities. See photograph opposite page 169.

makes about 750 ml/1¼ pts/1 large bottle

> 450 g/1 lb fresh or frozen raspberries, loganberries, blackberries or tayberries
>   (or a mixture of berries)
> 500 ml/17 fl oz/2¼ cups white wine or colourless distilled malt vinegar
> 450 g/1 lb/2 cups granulated sugar

1 Put the berries and vinegar in a 1.75 litre/3 pt/7½ cup capacity bowl and stir well. Cover with a plate or microwave wrap and leave to macerate for four days, stirring daily.

2 Strain the vinegar from the fruit into a 2.5 litre/4½ pt/11¼ cup capacity bowl and add the sugar. Discard the fruit. Cook the vinegar on Full (750–800w) for 15 minutes, stirring twice with a wooden spoon.

3 Leave to cool, then pour into a bottle and seal with a cork or a non-metallic lid.

4 Label and store in a cool, dark place almost indefinitely.

Simple Spiced Vinegar

A smooth vinegar that can be used for pickling.

makes 600 ml/1 pt/1 bottle

600 ml/1 pt/2½ cups distilled malt, colourless malt, dark malt or rice vinegar

15 ml/1 tbsp mixed pickling spice

2–3 fresh bird's eye chillies

7.5 ml/1½ tsp salt

30 ml/2 tbsp granulated sugar

6 cardamom pods, split open so that the seeds show

1 Put all the ingredients in a 1.2 litre/2 pt/5 cup capacity bowl and heat, uncovered, on Full (750–800w) for 8 minutes. Stir round once with a wooden spoon to dissolve the sugar completely.

2 Remove from the microwave, cover and leave to stand for 24 hours.

3 Strain the vinegar into a bottle and seal with a cork or a non-metallic lid.

4 Label and store in a cool, dark place almost indefinitely.

Spiced Pickling Vinegar

A full-flavoured vinegar for general pickling purposes and, where appropriate, for some of the pickles in this book (see pages 145–58). The amount of sugar you use will depend on how sweet you like your pickling vinegar.

makes 1.75 litres/3 pts/3 bottles

600 ml/1 pt/2½ cups boiling water
1.2 litres/2 pts/5 cups dark malt vinegar
45 ml/3 tbsp mixed pickling spice
2 bay leaves
2 dried red chillies
1 cinnamon stick
A sprig of dried thyme
15 ml/1 tbsp salt
100–175 g/4–6 oz/½–¾ cup granulated or soft light brown sugar

1 Put all the ingredients in a 2.25 litre/4 pt/10 cup capacity bowl, adding sugar to taste, and cook, uncovered, on Full (750–800w) for 5 minutes. Stir carefully with a wooden spoon until the sugar has dissolved completely.

2 Reduce the power to Medium (550w) and continue to cook, uncovered, for 25 minutes.

3 Remove from the microwave, cover and leave to stand for 24 hours.

4 Strain the vinegar into bottles and seal with a cork or a non-metallic lid.

5 Label and store in a cool, dark place almost indefinitely.

Spiced Garlic Pickling Vinegar

makes 1.75 litres/3 pts/3 bottles

Prepare as for Spiced Pickling Vinegar, but add 1–3 sliced garlic cloves to the ingredients before heating. Alternatively, you can use 2.5 ml/½ tsp of garlic granules or half plain and half garlic salt instead of all salt.

Mild Pickling Vinegar

makes 1.75 litres/3 pts/3 bottles

Prepare as for Spiced Pickling Vinegar, but increase the quantity of boiling water to 1.2 litres/2 pts/5 cups and reduce the quantity of vinegar to 900 ml/ 1 pt/2½ cups. Use light instead of dark malt vinegar.

Far Eastern-style Pickling Vinegar

A flavour-filled vinegar with a taste of Thailand. See photograph opposite page 169.

makes 1.2 litres/2 pts/2 bottles

1.2 litres/2 pts/5 cups colourless distilled malt vinegar
3 fresh bird's eye chillies
2 stems of lemon grass, halved lengthways
½ teacup fresh coriander (cilantro)
5 fresh lime leaves, torn in half
3 star anise
2 garlic cloves, halved
45 ml/3 tbsp caster sugar
5 ml/1 tsp salt
300 ml/½ pt/1¼ cups boiling water
1 walnut-sized piece of fresh root ginger, peeled and thickly sliced

1 Put all the ingredients in a 2.25 litre/4 pt/10 cup capacity bowl and heat for 10 minutes on Full (750–800w), stirring twice with a wooden spoon to dissolve the sugar completely.

2 Remove from the microwave, cover and leave to stand for 24 hours.

3 Strain into bottles and seal with a cork or a non-metallic lid.

4 Label and store in a cool, dark place almost indefinitely.

Mediterranean Herbed and Spiced Vinegar

Warm, colourful and charismatic, this makes a super success story in salad dressings and bastes.

makes 600 ml/1 pt/1 bottle

300 ml/½ pt/1¼ cups boiling water

450 ml/¾ pt/2 cups red wine vinegar

450 ml/¾ pt/2 cups fresh mint leaves, loosely packed

A walnut-sized piece of fresh root ginger, peeled and thickly sliced

1 cinnamon stick

10 ml/2 tsp salt

30 ml/2 tbsp granulated sugar

Thin strips of peel from ½ orange

1 Put all the ingredients in a 1.2 litre/2 pt/5 cup capacity bowl and cook on Full (750–800w) for 10 minutes, stirring twice with a wooden spoon to dissolve the sugar completely.

2 Remove from the microwave, cover and leave to stand for 24 hours.

3 Strain into a bottle and seal with a cork or a non-metallic lid.

4 Label and store in a cool, dark place almost indefinitely.

Flavoured Olives

All round the world, olives sit on restaurant and hotel bars along with peanuts and crisps and you either go for them in a big way or you don't. Because they are now considered such a top-notch food for good health, it could be that they're the most superior snack food of all and hopefully these recipes will urge you to be more adventurous with this wonderful fruit that goes back to biblical times.

Split Green Olives with Garlic and Coriander

Warmly flavoured with coriander (cilantro), garlic and lemon, these olives make a wonderful cocktail snack before a Balkan-style meal and you can often find them piled high on the delicatessen counters in Greek and Cypriot food shops. Try adding them to stews and casseroles of lamb and chicken, tossing them with robust salads or studding them into pizzas. Prepared at home, they have a fresh, zingy taste and keep well in the fridge.

makes 250 g/9 oz/1 small jar

> 225 g/8 oz green olives with stones (pits)
> 15 ml/1 tbsp coriander seeds
> 4 fresh lemon slices, quartered
> 2 garlic cloves, thinly sliced

1 Put all the ingredients in a roomy plastic food bag and tie loosely at the top with a non-metallic tie or a length of string. Stand the bag on a non-breakable surface and bash with a rolling pin until the olives split. Don't overdo it or you'll end up with pulped olives.

2 Microwave in the bag on Full (750–800w) for 30 seconds.

3 Transfer to a warmed jar, top with a paper disc, then a lid or cellophane and label the jar.

4 Store in the fridge for up to two weeks, but no longer or the olives may turn mouldy.

The oils in refrigerated jars may develop small white speckles: this is quite normal and is a sign of nothing more sinister than the cold and will disappear at room temperature.

Split Black Olives with Herbs and Orange

A piquant mix with a Spanish twist.

makes 250 g/9 oz/1 small jar

225 g/8 oz Greek kalamata black olives with stones (pits)
4 slices of orange
4 dried or fresh bird's eye chillies
5 ml/1 tsp freeze-dried mint
2 garlic cloves, sliced

1 Put all the ingredients in a roomy plastic food bag and tie loosely at the top with a non-metallic tie or a length of string. Stand the bag on a non-breakable surface and bash with a rolling pin until the olives split. Don't overdo it or you'll end up with pulped olives.

2 Microwave in the bag on Full (750–800w) for 30 seconds.

3 Transfer to a warmed jar, top with a paper disc, then a lid or cellophane and label the jar.

4 Store in the fridge for up to two weeks, but no longer or the olives may turn mouldy.

Mixed Party Olives with Herbs and Orange in Olive Oil

All three varieties of olives absorb the aromas of the herbs and oranges successfully, giving them a distinctive burst of flavour. Drain well before serving, and accompany with cocktail sticks (toothpicks) to stop fingers becoming oily. See photograph opposite.

makes 900 g/2 lb/1 large jar

150 g/5 oz Greek black olives with stones (pits)

150 g/5 oz Greek pink olives (also called black but lighter) with stones

150 g/5 oz large green queen olives with stones

2 sprigs of fresh marjoram

2 sprigs of fresh fennel

A small sprig of rosemary

2 sprigs of mint

4 fresh basil leaves

4 slices of orange

Good-quality olive oil (but not necessarily virgin)

1 Mix together the olives and herbs in a warmed jar. Push in 3 of the orange slices, then top up with olive oil. Leave uncovered and warm on Full (750–800w) for 2 minutes.

2 Add the remaining orange slice, then top with a paper disc and leave until cold.

3 Cover with a well-fitting lid or cellophane and label the jar.

4 Store in the fridge for up to three weeks.

Opposite: *Mixed Party Olives with Herbs and Orange in Olive Oil and Feta Cheese in Grapeseed Oil with Mixed Herbs, Garlic and Lemon (page 175)*

Green Olives with Caperberries, Chillies and Lemon

A sophisticated appetiser, you can also use this oil as a garnish on quiches and savoury flans, in salads and in earthy Italian or Spanish stews. The oil can be incorporated into French dressings and bastes. If you are serving the olives and caperberries with drinks, drain them thoroughly and serve with cocktail sticks (toothpicks) to prevent oily fingers.

makes 225 g/8 oz/1 small jar

175 g/6 oz smallish green olives with stones (pits)
40 g/1½ oz/approx. ½ cup bottled caperberries left on their stems
3 fresh lemon slices, quartered
4 dried or fresh bird's eye chillies
Grapeseed or olive oil

1 Toss all the ingredients together except the oil in a 1.2 litre/2 pt/5 cup capacity bowl. Warm through, uncovered, on Full (750–800w) for 1 minute 20 seconds.

2 Spoon into a warmed jar, fill up with oil, top with a paper disc and leave until cold.

3 Cover with a lid or cellophane and label the jar.

4 Store in the fridge for up to two weeks.

Opposite: *Fruit Vinegar (page 160) and Far Eastern-style Pickling Vinegar (page 163)*

Black Kalamata Olives in Grapeseed Oil with Garlic and Dill

Brilliant with Greek cheese, scrambled eggs and omelettes, these olives are also wonderful tossed with pasta. If you are serving the olives with drinks, drain them thoroughly and serve with cocktail sticks (toothpicks) to prevent oily fingers. The soaking is necessary because these olives are very salty.

makes 250 g/9 oz/1 small jar

225 g/8 oz black kalamata olives with stones (pits)
2 garlic cloves, sliced
7 g/¼ oz/1 cup fresh dill fronds
Grapeseed oil

1 Soak the olives for 2–3 hours in several changes of cold water. Drain thoroughly.

2 Layer in a 350 ml/12 fl oz/1½ cup capacity jar alternately with the garlic and dill. Cover with the grapeseed oil.

3 Leave uncovered and heat on Full (750–800w) for 1 minute. Top with a paper disc, then leave until cold.

4 Cover with a lid or cellophane and label the jar.

5 Store in the fridge up to three weeks.

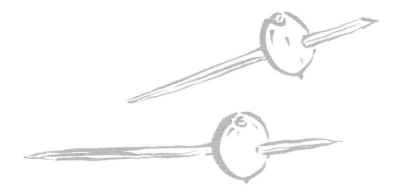

Stuffed Olive, Tomato and Herb Paste

A splendid, warm-hearted and piquant mix that can be put to so many uses: as a spread on crostini, a dip for vegetables, a sauce for spaghetti, a topping for pizza, and a flavoursome addition to stews and casseroles.

makes 700 g/1½ lb/2 small jars

400 g/14 oz stuffed olives
15 g/½ oz/1 cup fresh curly parsley
45 ml/3 tbsp chopped fresh dill (dill weed)
45 ml/3 tbsp chopped fresh mint
4 garlic cloves, sliced
75 ml/5 tbsp sun-dried tomato paste
150 ml/¼ pt/⅔ cup olive oil
15 ml/1 tbsp caster (superfine) sugar
Juice of 1 medium lemon
2.5 ml/½ tsp grated nutmeg

1 Put all the ingredients in a food processor or blender and work to a slightly grainy paste. (It should be neither too smooth nor too coarse.)

2 Transfer to a pottery, glass or plastic bowl suitable for the microwave, leave uncovered and heat on Medium (550w) for 1½ minutes.

3 Spoon into warmed jars, top with paper discs and leave until cold.

4 Cover with a lid or cellophane and label the jar.

5 Store in the fridge for up to three weeks.

Black Olive and Herb Paste

A variation on the previous recipe and for the same uses, the tastes in this olive paste are more intense and dramatic, with the faintest hint of heat from the Tabasco.

makes 700 g/1½ lb/2 small jars

400 g/14 oz black olives without stones (pits)

30 ml/2 tbsp frozen herbs for pasta or 10ml/2 tsp dried herbes de Provence

2 fresh sage leaves

75 ml/5 tbsp sun-dried tomato paste

10 ml/2 tsp bottled crushed garlic in sunflower oil

2.5–5 ml/½–1 tsp Tabasco sauce

15 ml/1 tbsp caster (superfine) sugar

10 ml/2 tsp Worcestershire sauce

150 ml/¼ pt/⅔ cup olive oil

1 Put all the ingredients in a food processor or blender and work to a slightly grainy paste. It should be neither too smooth nor too coarse.

2 Transfer to a pottery, glass or plastic bowl suitable for the microwave, leave uncovered and heat on Medium (550w) for 1½ minutes.

3 Spoon into warmed jars, top with paper discs and leave until cold.

4 Cover with a lid or cellophane and label the jar.

5 Store in the fridge for up to three weeks.

Cheeses in Oil

Beginning to appear in jars in food shops, cheeses in oil with additional flavourings are versatile, adaptable and delicious whether added to salads, eaten as part of a Middle Eastern *meze*, put on to rustic breads and grilled (broiled) or, with the oil, tossed into pasta, used as a pizza topping or a filling for jacket potatoes and pitta bread.

Mozzarella in Olive and Walnut Oils with Sage, Rosemary and Garlic

Although the cheese has a tendency to sink to the bottom of the jar, the cubes still hold their shape without sticking together, and absorb all the essential flavours and scents of the herbs and oils. Eat with green salads, using the oil to make a classy dressing. Spoon the cheese on to slices of hot, toasted Italian bread spread with tomato paste. Use the oil for basting roasted vegetables or for shallow-frying fillets of fish. Spoon the cheese out of the jar and eat with fresh figs, fresh apricots or persimmon to round off a meal.

makes 750 ml/1¼ pts/1 jar

250 g/9 oz Mozzarella cheese, cubed
3 garlic cloves, sliced
2 sage leaves
2 x 7.5 cm/2 x 3 in sprigs of rosemary
225 ml/8 fl oz/1 cup olive oil
50 ml/2 fl oz/¼ cup walnut oil
10 ml/2 tsp celery salt

1 Put the Mozzarella in a 750 ml/1¼ pt/3 cup capacity jar with the garlic, sage leaves and rosemary.

2 Pour the oils and celery salt into a measuring jug or small bowl. Leave uncovered and cook on Full (750–800W) for 2 minutes. Stir well.

3 Pour the oil into the jar over the cheese and herbs, top with a paper disc and leave until cold.

4 Cover with a lid or cellophane and label the jar.

5 Store in the fridge for up to four months.

Feta Cheese in Grapeseed Oil
with Mixed Herbs, Garlic and Lemon

Like a burst of Mediterranean sunshine, the cheese breaks on the scene with tempting pungency and is powerful stuff tucked into pitta bread with salad, used as a pizza topping with pepper antipasto or in a chunky sandwich with crisply fried (sautéed) bacon, anchovies and sliced stuffed olives. See photograph opposite page 168.

makes 750 ml/1¼ pts/1 jar

225 g/8 oz Feta cheese, cubed
1 spray of fresh fennel
1 x 7.5 cm/1 x 3 in sprig of mint
2 garlic cloves, each cut into 4 strips
1 lemon, halved and sliced
300 ml/½ pt/1¼ cups grapeseed oil

1 Put the Feta in a 750 ml/1¼ pt/3 cup capacity jar with the fennel, mint, garlic and lemon slices.

2 Pour the oil into a measuring jug or small bowl. Leave uncovered and heat on Full (750–800w) for 2 minutes. Stir well.

3 Pour the oil into the jar over the cheese, herbs and lemon, top with a paper disc and leave until cold.

4 Cover with a lid or cellophane and label the jar.

5 Store in the fridge for up to four months.

Spiced Halloumi Cheese in Mixed Oils

A strong and earthy combination, which suits this strong-tasting goats' or ewes' milk cheese down to the ground. Spoon both the oil and cheese over sliced tomatoes for a starter, or spoon over thick slices of seeded Greek or Turkish bread and toast under the grill (broiler) for a fast snack. Toasted sesame oil gives a delicious nutty flavour and is available in all good supermarkets.

makes 750 ml/1¼ pts/1 jar

> 250 g/9 oz Halloumi cheese, cubed
> 4 bay leaves
> 15 ml/1 tbsp mixed pickling spice
> 2 short stems of lemon balm OR 1 stem of lemon grass, trimmed and thinly sliced
> 250 ml/8 fl oz/1 cup sunflower oil
> 50 ml/2 fl oz/¼ cup toasted sesame oil

1 Put the Halloumi cheese in a 750 ml/1¼ pt/3 cup capacity jar with 2 of the bay leaves, the pickling spice and the lemon balm or lemon grass.

2 Pour the oils into a measuring jug or small bowl. Leave uncovered and cook on Full (750–800w) for 2 minutes. Stir well.

3 Pour the oil into the jar over the cheese and herbs. Top with the remaining bay leaves, then add a paper disc and leave until cold.

4 Cover with a lid or cellophane and label the jar.

5 Store in the fridge for up to four months.

Halloumi Cheese in Olive Oil
with Chilli, Capers and Tarragon

A surprisingly delicate yet sharpish mix, which is great in any kind of tossed salad with croûtons, eggs and avocado. You can also make the recipe with Feta cheese.

makes 750 ml/1¼ pts/1 jar

225 g/8 oz Halloumi cheese, cubed
2 x 15 cm/2 x 6 in sprigs of tarragon
30 ml/2 tbsp small and well-drained capers
13 cm/5 in long red chilli, cut into strips, seeds left in
25 ml/1½ tbsp hazelnut oil
25 ml/1½ tbsp walnut oil

1 Put the cheese in a 750 ml/1¼ pt/3 cup capacity jar with the tarragon, capers and chilli strips.

2 Pour the oils into a measuring jug or small bowl. Leave uncovered and heat on Full (750–800w) for 2 minutes. Stir well.

3 Pour the oils into the jar over the cheese and herbs, top with a paper disc and leave until cold.

4 Cover with a lid or cellophane the label the jar.

5 Store in the fridge for up to four months.

A World of Tastes

Now that so many more exciting ingredients are becoming available to adventurous cooks, we want to extend our repertoire of ingredients right round the globe. These exceptional home-made versions of various international preserves can be produced easily in your microwave.

Canadian-style Sweet Onion Confit

I brought this recipe home from Quebec in the mid-1980s. It was quite new then and had been served with rich pâté in a high-style restaurant in the trendiest part of the city. Now adopted by the culinary smart set cooks in Britain, it is sometimes referred to as marmalade. Besides pâté, it works brilliantly with cold meats like bacon and ham, with game pie and roasted guinea fowl.

makes 550 g/1¼ lb/1 large jar

450 g/1 lb white onions, finely chopped
25 g/1 oz/2 tbsp unsalted butter
5 ml/1 tsp olive oil
120 ml/¼ pt/⅔ cup chicken or vegetable stock
100 g/4 oz/½ cup caster (superfine) sugar
5 ml/1 tsp salt
1.5–2.5 ml/¼–½ tsp white pepper

1 Put all the ingredients in a 1.5 litre/2½ pt/6 cup capacity bowl. Leave uncovered and cook on Full (750–800w) for 20–22 minutes until the onion is tender, stirring three times with a wooden spoon.

2 Allow to cool to lukewarm, then ladle into a warmed jar, top with a paper disc and leave until cold.

3 Cover with a lid or cellophane and label the jar.

4 Store in the fridge for about two weeks. Alternatively, you can freeze the confit for up to three months in a suitable container with a well-fitting lid.

Red Onion Confit

makes 550 g/1¼ lb/1 large jar

Prepare as for Canadian-style Sweet Onion Confit, but use half red wine and half red wine vinegar instead of stock and substitute 150 g/5 oz/⅔ cup of soft light brown sugar for the caster (superfine) sugar. You can also use red onions instead of white.

Cape Malay Apricot Blatjang

A South African chutney-style condiment from the Cape, strongly Javanese in temperament from where it originated, and now eaten in the province with Far Eastern food, curries and chicken dishes. It's distinctly unusual and well worth a try.

makes 1 kg/2¼ lb/2 jars

450 g/1 lb/2⅔ cups dried apricots, snipped into small pieces
500 ml/17 fl oz/2¼ cups cold water
4 small fresh red chillies
5–6 garlic cloves, halved
225 g/8 oz onions, thickly sliced
10 ml/2 tsp salt
120 g/4 oz/½ cup soft dark brown sugar
150 ml/¼ pt/⅔ cup malt vinegar

1 Put the apricots and water in a 2.25 litre/4 pt/10 cup capacity bowl and leave to soak overnight.

2 Put the chillies, garlic and onions in a food processor and grind to a coarse paste. Add to the apricots and water.

3 Leave uncovered and cook on Full (750–800w) for 10 minutes, stirring twice with a wooden spoon.

4 Stir in all the remaining ingredients and continue to cook on Full, uncovered, for 25–30 minutes until thick, stirring three or four times.

5 Allow to cool to lukewarm, then ladle into warmed jars, top with paper discs and leave until cold.

6 Cover with non-metallic lids or cellophane and label the jars.

7 Store in a cool, dark place for up to six months.

Date Blatjang

makes 1 kg/2¼ lb/2 jars

Prepare as for Cape Malay Blatjang, but use a 450 g/1 lb block of cooking dates instead of the apricots and cook with mango juice instead of water. Increase the quantity of vinegar by 30 ml/2 tbsp.

Harissa

Imagine thinnish mayonnaise, the colour of salmon, satin smooth and with the heat of the devil and you come close to North Africa's harissa, a hot and unique flavouring sauce traditionally served with the country's national dish, couscous. Sometimes it appears with salads and, if thinned down with lemon juice, can be used as a fire-eater's baste for kebabs. Shop-bought versions are available in jars and cans but nothing quite matches the special taste of harissa you've made yourself.

makes 150 ml/¼ pt/1 small jar

3 garlic cloves, halved

1 medium red (bell) pepper, halved and seeded

4–6 dried bird's eye chillies

10 ml/2 tsp ground coriander (cilantro)

120 ml/4 fl oz/½ cup extra virgin olive oil

2.5 ml/½ tsp salt

1 Put all the ingredients in a 750 ml/1¼ pt/3 cup capacity bowl. Leave uncovered and heat on Low (250–300w) for 5 minutes.

2 Blend to a smooth paste in a blender or food processor.

3 Pack into a small jar, top with a paper disc and leave until cold.

4 Cover with a lid or cellophane and label the jar.

5 Store in the fridge for up to four weeks.

Indonesian Coconut and Peanut Sprinkle

Sprinkled over Indonesian and Malaysian foods, this particular mix is something I first came across and tried out over twenty years ago and it's worth its weight in gold. As a flavour and texture enhancer, it has originality and flair and keeps for many months in the cool, either in a lidded jar or in a plastic food bag. It's a pleasure tossed with salad greens, as a topping on freshly cooked rice and even mixed into yoghurt to make a dip. Galangal is a Far Eastern spice, pleasingly aromatic, with hints of pepper and ginger. You can buy it in major supermarkets and delicatessens.

makes 200 g/7 oz/1 small jar

15 ml/1 tbsp corn oil

50 g/2 oz/^{1}/$_2$ cup desiccated (shredded) coconut

75 g/3 oz/^{3}/$_4$ cup salted peanuts

1 shallot, chopped

3 garlic cloves, chopped

15 ml/1 tbsp bottled galangal with soya bean oil

2.5 ml/^{1}/$_2$ tsp ground cumin

5 ml/1 tsp light brown soft sugar

10 ml/2 tsp lemon juice

1 Put all the ingredients in a 1.2 litre/2 pt/5 cup capacity bowl and toss gently until thoroughly mixed.

2 Leave uncovered and cook on Full (750–800w) for 3^1/$_2$–4 minutes until toasted, stirring every minute. Watch all the time as coconut has a tendency to burn more quickly than one would expect, even in the microwave.

3 Allow to cool to lukewarm, then ladle into a warmed jar and leave until cold.

4 Cover with a lid and label the jar.

5 Store in a cool, dark place for up to two months.

Chunky Cranberry Sauce

A North American institution and a must with the Thanksgiving turkey, this condiment is now as much a part of the British Christmas meal as gravy and bread sauce.

makes 700 g/1 ½ lb/2 small jars

> 300 ml/½ pt/1¼ cups boiling water
> 225 g/8 oz/1 cup granulated sugar
> 450 g/1 lb cranberries

1 Put all the ingredients in a 1.75 litre/3 pt/ 7½ cup capacity bowl. Leave uncovered and cook on Full (750–800w) for 25–30 minutes until the sauce thickens and bubbles vigorously. Stir frequently with a wooden spoon for the first 10 minutes to make sure the sugar has dissolved, then stir twice or three times during the rest of the cooking time.

2 Spoon into warmed jars while still hot, then top with paper discs and leave until cold.

3 Cover with lids or cellophane and label the jars.

4 Store in a cool, dark place for up to six weeks.

Cranberry Sauce with Clementine

Makes 700 g/1 ½ lb/2 small jars

Prepare as for Chunky Cranberry Sauce, but add the finely grated (shredded) peel of 1 clementine at the beginning of cooking.

Plum Sauce with Sake

A distinctive and aristocratic sauce that makes the perfect accompaniment to Chinese food, especially duck.

makes 1 kg/2¼ lb/2 jars

900 g/2 lb dark and fleshy red plums, halved and stoned (pitted)
225 g/8 oz onions, finely chopped
10 ml/2 tsp mustard powder
300 ml/½ pt/1¼ cups Spiced Pickling Vinegar (see page 162)
225 g/8 oz/1 cup soft dark brown sugar
10 ml/2 tsp salt
45 ml/3 tbsp sake

1 Put the plums, onions, mustard and vinegar in a 2.25 litre/4 pt/10 cup capacity bowl. Cover and cook on Full (750–800w) for 8 minutes, stirring twice with a wooden spoon. Strain, reserving the liquid.

2 Pour the plum mixture into a blender or food processor and purée, then return it to the original bowl with the reserved liquid and add the sugar, salt and 30 ml/2 tbsp of the sake. Cover and leave to stand at room temperature for 6–8 hours.

3 Leave uncovered and cook on Full for 30 minutes, stirring several times.

4 Add the remaining sake. Allow to cool to lukewarm, then ladle into warmed jars, top with paper discs and leave until cold.

5 Cover with non-metallic lids or cellophane and label the jars.

6 Store in a cool, dark place for up to three months.

Preserved Lemons

North African and Middle Eastern, these salty lemons are zippy, palate-cleansing and sharp-tasting. They keep a long, long time in the cool and never lose their yellow brightness or their unique briny tang. Serve cut up into small pieces in a bowl of olives, eat little pieces with Feta cheese, toss squares into Mediterranean salads, use to garnish lamb couscous and tagines, add the liquid to salad dressings and bastes or brush it with oil over foods to be barbecued. The lemons are a useful investment and can even be added to tequila with chilled apple juice to make an original and trendy cocktail, Tequila Dawn.

makes about 1.5 kg/3 lb/1 very large jar

550 g/1¼ lb lemons, unwaxed if possible
150 g/5 oz/⅔ cup coarse sea salt
450–600 ml/¾–1 pt/2–2½ cups fresh lemon juice

1 Heat all but two of the lemons, two or three at a time, on Medium (550w) for 1 minute to soften them and make them easier to handle.

2 Leaving the tops and bottoms intact, cut downwards through each lemon, dividing them into six segments as though you were making Hallowe'en lanterns. Layer in a crock pot or very large jar with the salt. Cover loosely and leave untouched for 48 hours.

3 Cut the remaining lemons lengthways into 6 segments and add to the jar with enough lemon juice to reach the brim. Cover securely with several thicknesses of microwave wrap (plastic wrap) and leave in a cool, dark place for at least three months before using.

4 Store in a cool, dark place for several months.

Pepper Antipasto

Useful to have on hand as an appetiser or even a topping for pizza, the peppers are straightforward to prepare and have good storing qualities.

makes 900 g/2 lb/2 jars

700 g/1½ lb mixed coloured (bell) peppers
60 ml/4 tbsp olive or sunflower oil
4 sprigs of fresh oregano
8 garlic cloves, sliced
250 ml/8 fl oz/1 cup colourless distilled malt vinegar
7.5 ml/1½ tsp salt
20 ml/4 tsp caster (superfine) sugar

1 Place the peppers in a foil-lined grill (broiler) pan and coat heavily with the oil. Grill (broil) for 15–18 minutes until charred and blackened, turning at least three times. Switch off the grill but leave the peppers cooling where they are for 6 minutes before transferring to a plastic bag and leaving until cold.

2 Remove the peppers from the bag, peel off the skins and remove and discard the inside seeds. Cut the flesh into strips.

3 Divide the peppers between two 600 ml/1 pt/2½ cup jars with the oregano and garlic.

4 Mix the remaining ingredients in a 600 ml/1 pt/2½ cup measuring jug and heat on Medium (550w) for 4 minutes, stirring once with a wooden spoon.

5 Leave until completely cold, then pour into jars over the peppers. Top with paper discs, then cover with non-metallic lids or cellophane and label the jars.

6 Store in a cool, dark place for up to three months.

Duxelles

A French classic, this is intended to be treated as a flavour enhancer and colourant for rich, dark gravies, stews, soups, sauces and casseroles. It is based on mushrooms flavoured with onion and shallot and has always been held in high regard by both chefs and home cooks who prefer natural flavourings to anything from a bottle. To use, add it 15 ml/1 tbsp at a time until you achieve the right colour and flavour balance.

makes 700 g/1½ lb/2 small jars

700 g/1½ lb large mushrooms, finely chopped
1 small onion, finely chopped
2 shallots, finely chopped
10–15 ml/2–3 tsp Worcestershire sauce
2.5 ml/½ tsp ground allspice
7.5 ml/1½ tsp salt
15 ml/1 tbsp olive or grapeseed oil

1 Put the mushrooms, onion and shallots in a 2.25 litre/4 pt/10 cup capacity bowl and cook, uncovered, on Medium-low or Defrost (270–300w) for 30 minutes, stirring three or four times with a wooden spoon.

2 Leave to stand for 15 minutes.

3 Stir in the remaining ingredients and cook, uncovered, on Full (750–800w) for 14–15 minutes until the mixture is quite thick and no longer watery.

4 Leave until cold, then spoon into jars and top with paper discs. Cover with lids or cellophane and label the jars.

5 Store in the fridge for up to three weeks, or freeze in small quantities and use as required.

Index